Global Recession – Causes, Impacts and Remedies Series

Economic Crises as a Result of Distrust

GLOBAL RECESSION – CAUSES, IMPACTS AND REMEDIES SERIES

Recessions: Prospects and Developments
Nerea M. Pérez and June A. Ortega (Editors)
2009. ISBN: 978-1-60456-866-0

Financial Crisis in America
Raymund T. Ovanhouser (Editor)
2009. ISBN: 978-1-60692-191-3

Economic Crises as a Result of Distrust
Emilio Gullini (Editor)
2010. ISBN: 978-1-60741-355-4

GLOBAL RECESSION – CAUSES, IMPACTS AND REMEDIES SERIES

ECONOMIC CRISES AS A RESULT OF DISTRUST

EMILIO GULLINI
EDITOR

Nova Science Publishers, Inc.
New York

For permission to use material from this book please contact us:
Telephone 631-231-7269; Fax 631-231-8175
Web Site: http://www.novapublishers.com

LIBRARY OF CONGRESS CATALOGING-IN-PUBLICATION DATA

Economic crises as a result of distrust / editor, Emilio Gullini.
p. cm.
Includes index.
ISBN 978-1-60741-355-4 (softcover)
1. Financial crises. 2. International finance. 3. Global Financial Crisis, 2008-2009. I. Gullini, Emilio.
HB3722.E275 2009
338.5'42--dc22
2009041025

Published by Nova Science Publishers, Inc. ✢ New York

TABLE OF CONTENTS

PREFACE

A large and relatively unimpeded flow of credit through healthy financial markets is a salient attribute of the U.S. economy and any well functioning modern economy. Banks and other financial institutions channel the economy's savings toward a variety of current productive uses. By borrowing short-term and lending long-term, these institutions create a flow of credit that passes liquidity from savers to investors, and transforms liquid short-run assets into less liquid long-term assets. But lending in credit markets requires confidence in the borrowers' ability to repay the debt (principal and interest) in full and on schedule. The current turmoil in U.S. financial markets is the result of a breakdown in that necessary confidence. In an environment of distrust, financial institutions are far less willing and able to lend long-term. This book examines the monetary policy and macro-economic supply factors in U.S. credit markets that contributed to the credit expansion. This book also defines credit default swaps, explains their use by banks for risk management, and discusses the potential for systemic risk. This book consists of public documents which have been located, gathered, combined, reformatted, and enhanced with a subject index, selectively edited and bound to provide easy access.

Chapter 1 - For a decade prior to 2005, the People's Republic of China (PRC) pegged its currency, the renminbi, to the U.S. dollar. On July 21 of that year, the PRC finally broke this peg. However, the PRC has continued to intervene heavily in foreign exchange markets to limit the subsequent appreciation of the renminbi. Governments in other Asian economies have sought to limit the appreciation of their currencies against both the renminbi and the U.S. dollar to maintain the price competitiveness of their manufactured exports with their Chinese rivals in North American and European markets. Shadowing the PRC's exchange rate policy, other Asian governments have also intervened heavily in foreign exchange markets. From 2001 to 2007, the PRC, India, Indonesia, Japan, South Korea, Malaysia, Taiwan, and Thailand have collectively added $2.7 trillion to their foreign exchange reserves. About 2/3 of these reserves have been invested in U.S. dollar-denominated assets, primarily U.S. Treasury and agency debt securities.

Since 2000, the PRC's exchange rate policy and the shadow policies of other Asian governments slowed the depreciation of the U.S. dollar and lowered interest rates, particularly at the long end of the yield curve. By distorting market price signals, these policies have exacerbated a number of economic problems not only in the United States but also around the world:

Chapter 2 - Chile experienced a banking crisis from 1981-84 that in relative terms had a cost comparable in size to that perhaps facing the United States today. The Chilean Central Bank acted quickly and decisively in three ways to restore faith in the credit markets. It restructured firm and household loans, purchased nonperforming loans temporarily, and facilitated the sale or liquidation of insolvent financial institutions. These three measures increased liquidity in the credit markets and restored the balance sheets of the viable financial institutions. The Central Bank required banks to repurchase the nonperforming loans when provision for their loss could be made and prohibited distribution of profits until they had all been retired. Although the private sector remained engaged throughout the resolution of this crisis, the fiscal costs were, nonetheless, very high.

The U.S. Congress is contemplating a $700 billion government assistance package to arrest the financial crisis in the United States. President Bush argued that failure to enact legislation quickly could result in a wholesale failure of the U.S. financial sector. As discussion of the Administration's plan unfolded, however, questions in Congress arose over issues of magnitude and management of the "bailout," the need for oversight, and the possibility that less costly and perhaps more effective alternatives might be available.

In this light, Chile's response to its 1981-84 systemic banking crisis has been held up as one example. The cost was comparable relative to the size of its economy to that facing the U.S. Government today. In 1985, Central Bank losses to rescue financially distressed financial institutions were estimated to be 7.8% of GDP[1] (equivalent to approximately $1 trillion in the United States today). The policy options Chile chose had similarities as well as differences from those contemplated in the United States today. Their relevance is debatable, but they do highlight an approach that succeeded in eventually stabilizing and returning the Chilean banking sector to health, while keeping the credit markets functioning throughout the crisis.

Chapter 3 - In the early 1990s, Sweden faced a banking and exchange rate crisis that led it to rescue banks that had experienced large losses on their balance sheets and that threatened a collapse of the banking system. Some analysts and others argue that Sweden's experience could provide useful lessons for the execution and implementation of the Emergency Economic Stabilization Act of 2008[1]. The banking crisis facing the United States is unique, so there are no exact parallels from which to draw templates. Sweden's experience, however, represents a case study in how a systemicbankingcrisis was resolved in a developed country with democratic institutions. The Swedish central bank separated out good assets, which it left to the banks to oversee from bad assets, which it placed in a separate agency with broad authority to work out debt problems or to liquidate assets. Four lessons that emerged form Sweden's experience are: 1) the process must be transparent; 2) the resolution agency must be politically and financially independent; 3) market discipline must be maintained; and 4) there must be a plan to jump-start credit flows in the financial system. This chapter provides an overview of the Swedish banking crisis and an explanation of the measures Sweden used to restore its banking system to health.

Chapter 4 - A large and relatively unimpeded flow of credit through healthy financial markets is a salient attribute of the U.S. economy and any well functioning modern economy. Banks and other financial institutions channel the economy's savings toward a variety of current productive uses. By borrowing short-term and lending long-term, these institutions create a flow of credit that passes liquidity from savers to investors, and transforms liquid short-run assets into less liquid long-term assets. These long-term assets are created by credit-financed, current spending by households on housing, consumer durables, and education, and by, current spending by businesses on new plant and equipment. But lending in credit markets requires confidence in the borrowers' ability to repay the debt (principal and interest) in full and on schedule. The current turmoil in U.S. financial markets is the result of a breakdown in that necessary confidence. In an environment of distrust, financial institutions are far less willing and able to lend long-term. The move toward short-term lending diminishes the flow of long-term credit to the non-financial economy and dampens the economic activities of households and businesses that are dependent on borrowing. Economic policy may be needed to get credit flowing smoothly again and to mitigate the damage incurred by households and non-financial businesses. A number of indicators have pointed to a substantial rise in the cost of credit and a decrease in the flow of credit to the broader economy.

A reduced flow of credit will likely dampen economic activity that is dependent on such borrowing as residential investment spending (purchasing new homes) by households, business investment spending (purchasing new plant and equipment) and consumer spending (purchasing autos, appliances, and higher education) by households. Residential investment spending has fallen over 40%

between the fourth quarter of 2005 and the third quarter of 2008, and has on average subtracted about 1.0 percentage point from real GDP growth in each of those six quarters. Non-residential investment spending continued to increase in 2007 and the first half of 2008, but the pace fell steadily, and in the third quarter of 2008 it declined 0.1%. Consumption expenditures had been increasing, but at a decelerating rate in 2007 and the first half of 2008. However, in the third quarter of 2008 consumer spending fell 3.1%. A recent study estimates that the decrement to the U.S. economy's supply of credit is about $1 trillion, leading to a potential drag on real GDP of about 1.8 percentage points for two years.

There are three types of policy response, applied separately or in combination as the severity of the problem warrants. The first type is the conventional macroeconomic policy tools of monetary and fiscal policy, used with the aim of broadly supporting bank liquidity and aggregate spending. Monetary policy, having greater flexibility than fiscal policy, will usually play the prominent role. The second type of policy for responding to a credit crisis is the Fed's traditional role of "lender of last resort," typically involving some expanded use of the Fed's discount window, the facility the Fed uses to make short term loans to banks that need to bridge a short-run shortage of liquidity. These policies will be more narrowly focused on the needs of troubled institutions. The third type of policy response is the use of "extraordinary measures" involving direct interventions by the federal government to restore confidence in financial markets, forcing credit to flow broadly and at greater volume.

Chapter 5 - During the week of September 13-20, 2008, the United States confronted the worst global financial crisis in almost a century. Credit markets, which are the circulatory system of the U.S. economy, seized up. The Federal Reserve was unable to revive credit markets through massive liquidity injections. Share prices plummeted, and a run began on money market mutual funds.

Federal Reserve Chairman Ben Bernanke and Secretary of the Treasury Henry Paulson determined that the *ad hoc* approach that the federal government had been taking to resolve this crisis was not working. Instead, the federal government needed a comprehensive plan that would resolve the uncertainty about value of impaired mortgage- related financial assets and the solvency of financial institutions holding these assets.

Secretary Paulson asked Congress to authorize the Treasury to purchase and liquidate up to $700 billion of impaired financial assets from financial institutions. Both credit and equity markets had a favorable initial response, but the subsequent reaction was less positive.

Chapter 6 - Macroeconomic and microeconomic policy blunders by both the U.S. government and foreign governments inflated an unsustainable housing bubble in the United States and other developed economies. When this bubble inevitably popped, a global financial crisis ensued. Although misaligned private incentives, methodological errors in rating structured credit products, and the recklessness of some private financial institutions and investors did play a contributory role in the recent financial turmoil, individuals and firms could not have created and sustained such a large housing bubble over so long a time without major macroeconomic and microeconomic policy mistakes.

Chapter 7 - The popping of the housing bubble, the subsequent increases in residential mortgage loan delinquency and foreclosure rates, and the recent failures of commercial and investment banks have prompted some Americans to suggest that current economic policies are similar to Herbert Hoover's.

To assess the validity of this assertion, one must first understand what Hoover's economic policies actually were. There is a widespread misconception that under Hoover the federal government remained idle as the economy contracted. In reality, Hoover aggressively pursued bad economic policies that transformed what could have been at worst a short recession into the worst depression in U.S. history.

Although Hoover did not understand banking, finance, and monetary policy, his success as an engineer, entrepreneur, and government official prior to his inauguration convinced him that he did not require economic advice. Hoover thought that he already knew everything that there was to know about economics. Hoover's arrogance proved disastrous. Hoover repeatedly ignored sound advice from prominent economists to pursue relentlessly bad economic policies based on his wrong-headed notions, his quirky morality, and his anti-bank, anti-Wall Street prejudices.

Chapter 8 - An unprecedented U.S. housing bubble began to inflate in the first quarter of 1998 and then popped in the second quarter of 2006. The subsequent deflation of housing prices has caused the delinquency and foreclosure rates for subprime residential mortgage loans to soar. Investors grew uncertain about the value of the residential mortgage-backed securities (RMBS) and the collateralized mortgage obligations (CMOs) into which many subprime residential mortgage loans had been placed. Consequently, the market liquidity for these subprime-related derivative securities shriveled.

Chapter 9 - This chapter explains how weakness in the U.S. housing sector morphed into a global financial crisis that began last August. Using the framework for analyzing asset bubbles that was introduced in a previous report,[1] this chapter examines stage two – credit expansion (microeconomic factors related to financial services) and stage six – financial panic and crisis management.

Chapter 10 - We are all familiar with the numerous ways in which we use credit. Credit finances the smaller purchases we make when we use our credit cards, and the larger purchases that are fundamental to our lives – the cars we drive, the homes we live in, the colleges where we send our children. Credit is also crucial for the needs of businesses, and for state and local governments.

Chapter 11 - Japan experienced large asset price bubbles in its stock and commercial real estate markets during the second half of the 1980s. These bubbles peaked in 1989 and 1990, respectively. Subsequently, both Japanese share prices and land values fell, surrendering all of their gains during the bubble years by 1993 and 2000, respectively.

After these bubbles popped, real GDP growth slowed abruptly. However, a series of fiscal and monetary blunders by the Japanese government transformed the inevitable post-bubble recession into a "lost decade" of deflation and stagnation. U.S. policymakers can learn valuable lessons of what to do and not to do by studying these blunders.

Chapter 12 - Credit default swaps are contracts that provide protection against default by third parties, similar to insurance. These financial derivatives are used by banks and other financial institutions to manage risk. The rapid growth of the derivatives market, the potential for widespread credit defaults (such as defaults for subprime mortgages), and operational problems in the over-the-counter (OTC) market where credit default swaps are traded, have led some policymakers to inquire if credit default swaps are a danger to the financial system and the economy. For example, the establishment of a conservatorship for the government sponsored enterprises (GSEs), Fannie Mae and Freddie Mac, in September 2008 potentially triggered credit default swap contracts with notional value exceeding $1.2 trillion. Processing and covering these commitments may be difficult. This chapter defines credit default swaps, explains their use by banks for risk management, and discusses the potential for systemic risk.

In: Economic Crises as a Result of Distrust
Editors: Emilio Gullini
ISBN: 978-1-60741-355-4

Chapter 1

CHINESE FOREIGN EXCHANGE INTERVENTIONS

Jim Saxton

EXECUTIVE SUMMARY

For a decade prior to 2005, the People's Republic of China (PRC) pegged its currency, the renminbi, to the U.S. dollar. On July 21 of that year, the PRC finally broke this peg. However, the PRC has continued to intervene heavily in foreign exchange markets to limit the subsequent appreciation of the renminbi. Governments in other Asian economies have sought to limit the appreciation of their currencies against both the renminbi and the U.S. dollar to maintain the price competitiveness of their manufactured exports with their Chinese rivals in North American and European markets. Shadowing the PRC's exchange rate policy, other Asian governments have also intervened heavily in foreign exchange markets. From 2001 to 2007, the PRC, India, Indonesia, Japan, South Korea, Malaysia, Taiwan, and Thailand have collectively added $2.7 trillion to their foreign exchange reserves. About 2/3 of these reserves have been invested in U.S. dollar-denominated assets, primarily U.S. Treasury and agency debt securities.

Since 2000, the PRC's exchange rate policy and the shadow policies of other Asian governments slowed the depreciation of the U.S. dollar and lowered interest rates, particularly at the long end of the yield curve. By distorting market price signals, these policies have exacerbated a number of economic problems not only in the United States but also around the world:

- These policies have contributed to the growth of unsustainable imbalances in the international accounts of both the PRC and the United States.
- The PRC's massive accumulation of foreign exchange reserves is stoking rapidly rising inflation in China.
- Low long-term interest rates contributed to the housing price bubble during the first half of this decade. As the bubble approached its peak, reckless lending became rampant.
- The bursting of this bubble revealed significant overinvestment and malinvestment in housing in the United States as well as significant speculative excesses in credit markets around the world.
- The inevitable unwinding of these imbalances, the liquidation of overinvestment and malinvestment in housing, and the restoration of confidence in credit markets may slow real GDP growth in the United States for several years.

I. Introduction

During the 1980s and 1990s, the foreign exchange value of the U.S. dollar was largely determined by the market-based, wealth-maximizing decisions of households and firms both here and abroad. Since 2000, however, the strategic interventions by central banks in foreign exchange markets have played a far larger role in determining the foreign exchange value of the U.S. dollar than during the two previous decades. In the last five years, the value of the U.S. dollar has declined (see Graph 1).

For a decade prior to 2005, the People's Republic of China (PRC) pegged its currency, the renminbi,[1] to the U.S. dollar. On July 21 of that year, the PRC broke this peg and finally allowed the value of its currency to rise, but not to a market-determined level. The People's Bank of China (PBC) continued to intervene heavily in foreign exchange markets to limit the subsequent appreciation of the renminbi. Governments in other developing and newly industrializing economies in northeast, southeast, and south Asia feared that significant appreciations of their currencies would cause their manufactured exports to lose their price competitiveness with their Chinese rivals in North American and European markets. Consequently, these governments have sought to limit the appreciation of their currencies against both the renminbi and the U.S. dollar.

Shadowing the PRC's exchange rate policy, the central banks in other Asian economies have also intervened heavily in foreign exchange markets since 2000. From 2001 to 2007, central banks in China, India, Indonesia, Japan, South Korea, Malaysia, Taiwan, and Thailand added $2.7 trillion to their foreign exchange reserves. About 2/3 of these reserves have been invested in U.S. dollar-denominated assets, primarily U.S. Treasury and agency debt securities.[2]

Since 2000, the PRC's exchange rate policy and the shadow policies of other Asian governments have kept dollar-denominated interest rates low, particularly at the long end of the yield curve, in the United States and to a lesser extent in Australia, Canada, and Europe. These policies also slowed the depreciation in the foreign exchange value of the U.S. dollar. Without massive interventions by the PRC and other Asian governments, long-term interest rates in the United States would have been significantly higher, and the foreign exchange value of the U.S. dollar would have been even lower.

By distorting market price signals, the PRC's exchange rate policy and the shadow policies of other Asian governments have exacerbated a number of economic problems not only in the United States but also around the world:

- These policies have contributed to the growth of unsustainable imbalances in the international accounts of both the PRC and the United States.[3]
- The PRC's massive accumulation of foreign exchange reserves is stoking rapidly rising inflation in China.
- Low long-term interest rates contributed to a housing price bubble in the United States. As the bubble approached its peak in 2006, reckless lending became rampant.
- The bursting of this bubble revealed significant overinvestment and malinvestment in housing in the United States as well as significant speculative excesses in credit markets around the world [4]
- The inevitable unwinding of these imbalances, the liquidation of overinvestment and malinvestment in housing, and the restoration of confidence in credit markets may slow real GDP growth in the United States for several years.

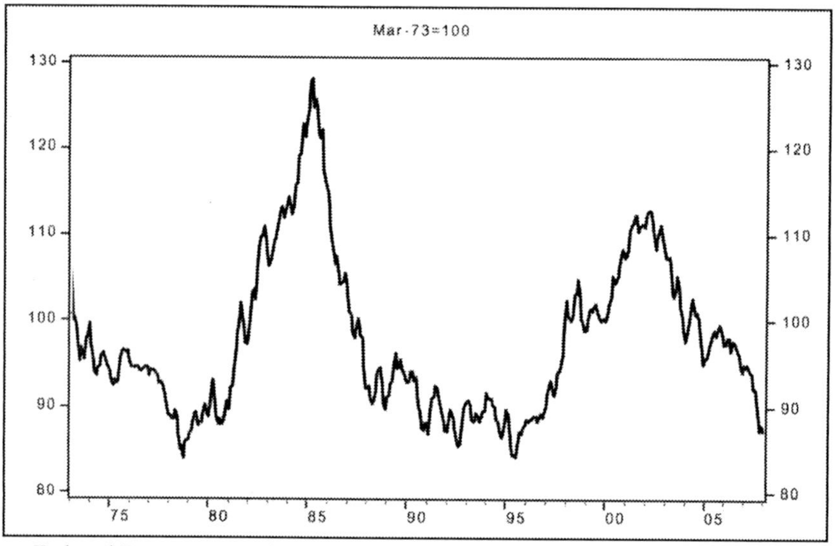

Source: Feder al Reserve Board /Haver Analytics

Graph 1. Real Broad Trade-Weighted Exchange Value of the US$

II. How Economic Factors Determine Exchange Rates and International Accounts

Under the Bretton Woods system (1945 to 1971), exchange rates were fixed. Current account transactions such as payments for imported goods were generally unregulated, but capital controls restricted both inward and outward investment transactions. International imbalances were resolved mainly through official flows of gold or U.S. dollars among central banks.

In 1973, the United States and other developed countries allowed market forces to determine the foreign exchange value of their currencies. Economists refer to this system as floating exchange rates. Over the next decade, developed and many developing countries abolished capital controls, freeing their residents to make outward foreign investment and opening their economies to inward foreign investment. In recent decades, international imbalances have been resolved mainly through market-determined changes in exchanges rates. Under floating exchange rates, a government may affect the foreign exchange value of its currency (1) through domestic monetary policy or (2) through its fiscal, regulatory, tax, trade, and other economic policies. Domestic monetary policy determines the supply of money. Changes in this supply relative to international demand affect the exchange rates of one currency with other currencies. Other economic policies affect the international demand for a country's currency by changing market expectations for the risk-adjusted after-tax rate of return. Since foreign residents must exchange their currencies to invest in other countries, policies that increase the expected risk-adjusted after-tax rate of return in one country will increase the foreign exchange value of its currency, and vice versa.

Exchange rates are also affected by the monetary policy decisions of foreign governments. If a foreign central bank were to increase the money supply of its currency faster than the growth in demand for its currency while the Federal Reserve kept the supply of U.S. dollars in line with the demand for U.S. dollars, then the exchange rate of the U.S. dollar is likely to appreciate against this foreign currency.

A policy-induced shift in either the supply of a country's currency or its international demand also changes such country's international accounts. An increase in inward foreign direct and portfolio investment will increase a country's capital and financial surplus (or reduce its deficit). This change automatically causes a country's current account deficit to increase (or its surplus to fall). Usually, this occurs through an increase in a country's trade deficit (or a decrease in its surplus) as the higher foreign exchange value of this country's currency simultaneously increases export prices in terms of other currencies and decreases import prices in terms of its own currency.

Between 1973 and 2000, official interventions by the U.S. Treasury and foreign central banks were limited and did not have a sustained influence on exchange rates. Portfolio investors can buy or sell financial assets almost instantaneously with minimal transaction costs to seek higher risk-adjusted after-tax returns, while trade and direct investment transactions often involve long-term contracts and commitments. Consequently, portfolio investment transactions by private households and firms rather than trade transactions or direct investment transactions have generally driven exchange rate fluctuations.

Both the disinflationary monetary policy pursued by the Federal Reserve and the Reagan administration policies of deregulation and marginal tax rate reductions increased expectations for higher risk-adjusted after-tax rates of return on U.S. investments. This drove a surge of inward private foreign investment in the early 1980s that increased the real foreign exchange value of the U.S. dollar. Again in the late 1990s, a high technology boom, trade liberalization, and a capital gains tax reduction drove another surge of inward private foreign investment, boosting the real foreign exchange value of the U.S. dollar. After these portfolio reallocations toward U.S. dollar-denominated assets peaked in 1985 and 2002, the real foreign exchange value of the U.S. dollar fell (see Graph 1).

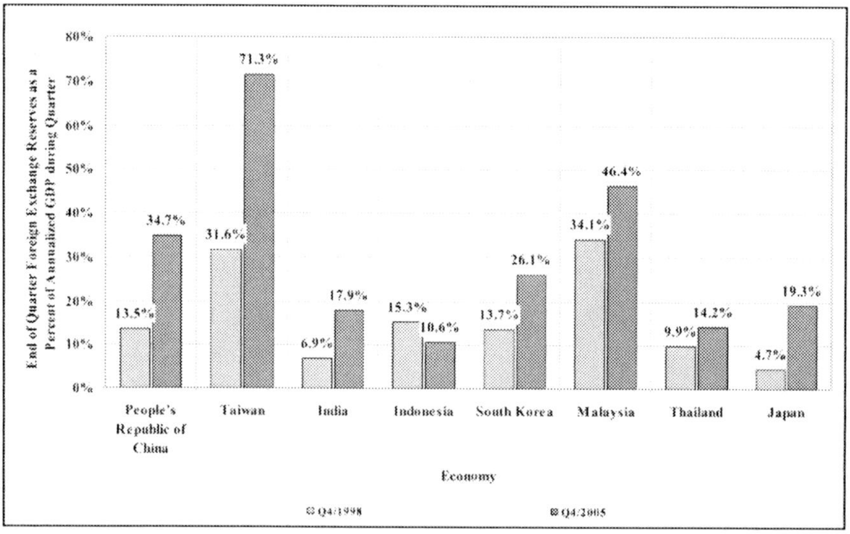

Graph 2A. Accumulation of Large Foreign Exchange Reserves in Asia

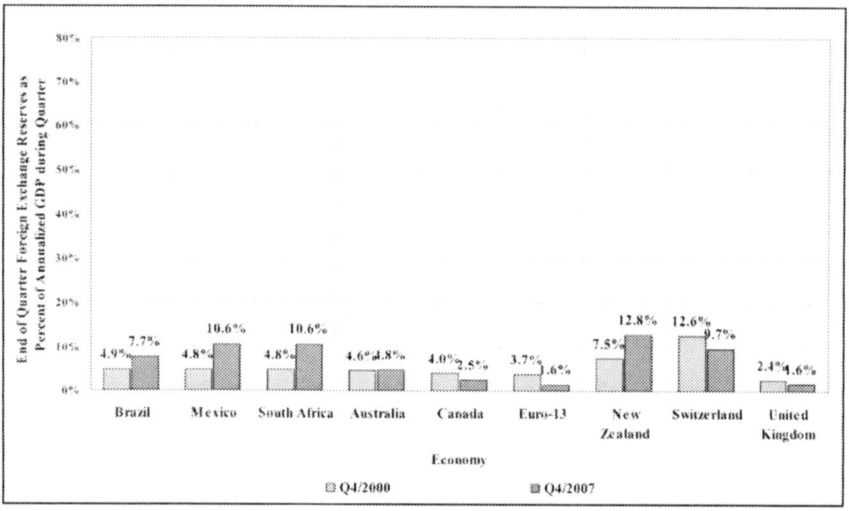

Graph 2B. Moderate Changes in Foreign Exchange Reserves in Major Developed and Developing Economies Outside of Asia

III. Massive Intervention Since 2000

After 2000, official transactions by the People's Bank of China and central banks in other Asian economies exerted significant upward pressure on the foreign exchange value of the U.S. dollar to keep the prices of their exports competitive. The PBC pegged the renminbi to the U.S. dollar through July 20, 2005, and thereafter allowed the renminbi to appreciate very gradually against the U.S. dollar. To maintain this peg and then to keep the renminbi from appreciating more rapidly to a market-determined level, China intervened heavily in foreign exchange markets by buying dollars and selling yuan. The PRC's foreign exchange reserves ballooned by $1.363 trillion since December 31, 2000 to $1.528 trillion on December 31, 2007. At year-end, the PRC's foreign exchange reserves were 34.7 percent of GDP (see Graph 2A). To contain the inflationary effects of issuing so many yuan, the PBC has tried to sterilize its foreign exchange interventions by issuing yuan-denominated bonds and increasing the reserve requirements for Chinese banks and other depository institutions. The PBC has used its dollars to purchase foreign debt securities, about two-thirds of which are believed to be U.S. dollar-denominated.

Fearing a loss of the price competitiveness of their exports, central banks in other Asian economies have intervened in foreign exchange markets to prevent a significant appreciation of their currencies against the renminbi. From December 31, 2000 to December 31, 2007, the foreign exchange reserves grew by $164 billion in Taiwan, $543 billion in India, Indonesia, South Korea, Malaysia, and Thailand combined, and $601 billion in Japan. Thus, central banks in China, India, Indonesia, Japan, South Korea, Malaysia, Taiwan, and Thailand have collectively added $2,671 billion to their foreign exchange reserves.

Graph 2A also shows how other Asian economies accumulated large foreign exchange reserves relative to their GDP from year-end 2000 to year-end 2007. On December 31, 2007, foreign exchange reserves totaled $270 billion in Taiwan, $763 billion in India, Indonesia, South Korea, Malaysia, and Thailand combined, and $948 billion in Japan.

These interventions have slowed the decline in the U.S. dollar that would have otherwise occurred. From July 20 2005 to February, 15, 2008, the U.S. dollar depreciated by 13.3 percent against the renminbi. However, this change reflects mostly a general decline in the nominal trade-weighted foreign exchange value of the U.S. dollar of 12.8 percent rather than a general appreciation in the foreign exchange value of the renminbi against other currencies (see Graph 3).

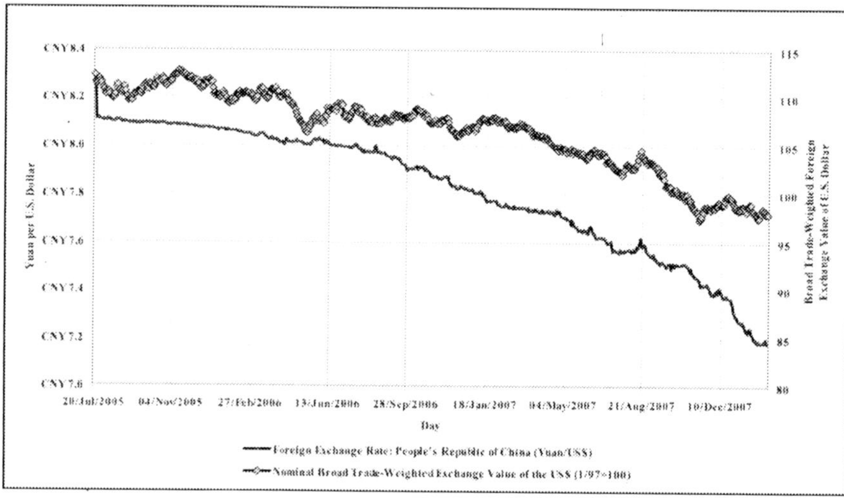

Graph 3. Change in Renminbi-U.S. Dollar Exchange Rate Reflects Broad Depreciation in Foreign Exchange Value of U.S. Dollar, Not Appreciation of Renminbi

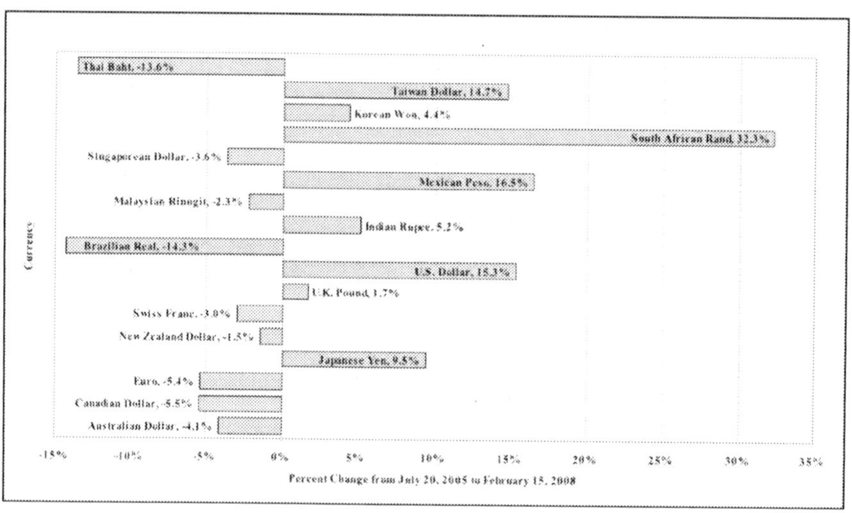

Graph 4. Changes in Exchange Rates of Major Developed, Major Developing, and other Asian Currencies against the Renminbi (July 20, 2005 to February 15, 2008)

In contrast, major developed and developing economies outside of Asia have not accumulated excessive foreign exchange reserves (see Graph 2B). From July 20, 2005 to February 15, 2008, the renminbi has appreciated by 15.3 percent against the U.S. dollar. During the same period, however, the renminbi has appreciated by much less against the British pound (1.7 percent) and the Japanese yen (9.5 percent). The renminbi depreciated by 5.5 percent against the Canadian dollar, 5.4 percent against the euro, 4.1 percent against the Australian dollar, 3.0 percent against the Swiss franc, and 1.5 percent against the New Zealand dollar (see Graph 4).

Except for the Thai baht, the shadow interventions by central banks in other developing and newly industrializing economies in Asia have kept their currencies broadly in line with the renminbi. Between July 20, 2005 and February 15, 2008, the renminbi has appreciated by 5.2 percent against the Indian rupee and 4.4 percent against the Korean won, while the renminbi has depreciated against the Malaysian rinngit by 2.3 percent and the Singaporean dollar by 3.6 percent (see Graph 4).

There is wide agreement among economists that the renminbi is severely undervalued. Earlier this year, Morris Goldstein, a senior fellow at the Peterson Institute for International Economics, reported that the renminbi "is now grossly under-valued – on the order of 30 percent or more against an average of China's trading partners and 40 percent or more against the U.S. dollar."[5]

The PRC's intervention and the shadow interventions by other Asian economies have boosted the international demand for the U.S. dollar, increasing its foreign exchange value and exacerbating international imbalances. The PRC's current account surplus rose from 1.3 percent of GDP in 2001 to 9.0 percent of GDP in 2006. Global Insight forecasts that the PRC's current account surplus will be at least 9.1 percent of GDP for 2007. The U.S. current account deficit grew from 3.8 percent of GDP in 2001 to 6.2 percent of GDP in 2006, before falling to a seasonally adjusted annualized level of 5.1 percent in the third quarter of 2007.

The PBC and other Asian central banks have invested their foreign exchange reserves heavily in U.S. Treasury debt securities and U.S. Agency debt securities. As of September 30, 2007, 53 percent of all privately held U.S. Treasuries were owned by foreign residents.[6] About 70 percent of these foreign residents are, in fact, foreign government agencies, mainly central banks in east, southeast, and south Asia and sovereign wealth funds (SWFs) in oil-exporting countries in the Middle East.

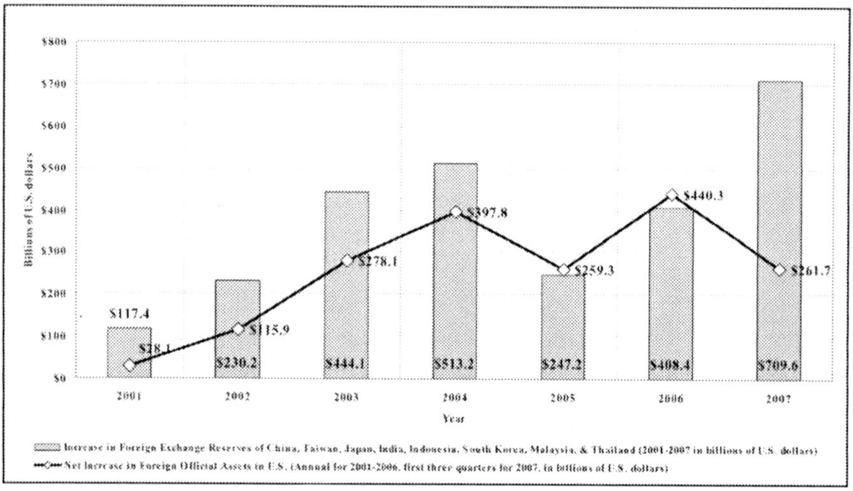

Graph 5. Annual Increase in Foreign Exchange Reserves and Change in Foreign Official Assets in the United States

This is a significant swing toward foreign ownership since December 31, 2000, when only 37 percent of all privately held U.S. Treasuries were owned by foreign residents. This swing is mainly attributable to a large increase in annual net purchases of U.S. securities by foreign governments from $28 billion (equal to 0.3 percent of GDP) in 2001 to $440 billion (equal to 3.3 percent of GDP) in 2006. Thus, the PBC's intervention and the shadow interventions by central banks in other Asian economies largely explain the spike in net purchases of U.S. securities by foreign governments during this period (see Graph 5).

IV. Economic Consequences

The PRC's exchange rate policy and its shadow policies in other Asian economies have enormous consequences for the United States and the rest of the world. These exchange rate manipulations have distorted prices and sent faulty signals to individuals and firms around the world.

A. Effects on China

- The PRC's exchange rate policy has reduced the real price of Chinese labor relative to labor in other countries. By lowering labor costs, the PRC encouraged a surge of inward direct investment by foreign multinational corporations (MNCs) in the labor-intensive manufacturing of low-tech goods and the final assembly of medium-tech consumer goods from imported parts. The rapid increase in both exports and imports by Chinese subsidiaries of foreign MNCs has driven the phenomenal growth of China's international trade.
- This exchange rate policy slowed the appreciation of the renminbi and the decline in the prices of imported goods and services in yuan terms. Consequently, Chinese households consume far fewer imported goods and services than they would without this intervention. Shadow exchange rate policies have also slowed the growth of domestic consumption of imported goods and services in other Asian economies.
- The PRC's exchange rate policy has effectively created a price ceiling known as the "China price" that severely limits the ability of manufacturers of labor-intensive goods in other countries to increase their prices and remain competitive.

B. Effects on the United States

- The China price has had disinflationary effects around the world.
- Because of the PRC's distortion of world prices, U.S. exports were lower and U.S. imports were higher than they would otherwise have been. Consequently, U.S. output and employment in the tradable goods and services sector were lower than they would otherwise have been.
- The massive interventions by the PBC and central banks in other Asian economies have tended to reduce long-term interest rates in the United States both directly and indirectly since 2000. First, the PBC and other Asian central banks bid-down U.S. interest rates through their massive purchases of U.S. dollar-denominated debt securities. Second, the China price effect has slowed the increase in various price indices that are used to measure inflation. As a result, inflation and inflationary expectations have been contained. This has allowed the Federal Reserve and other central banks outside of Asia to pursue more accommodative monetary policies that have also helped to keep long-term interest rates low.

- By lowering long-term interest rates, the exchange rate policies of the PRC and other Asian economies deterred investment in the United States and other economies in parts of the tradable goods sector in which Chinese firms and Chinese subsidiaries of foreign MNCs are highly competitive and encouraged investment in non-tradable sectors, especially housing. Thus, these policies contributed to the inflation of a housing price bubble in the United States that peaked in 2006. As the bubble expanded, builders constructed too many new units, and too many households borrowed more than they could reasonably afford in order to buy homes. After the bubble burst, some of this residential investment has been revealed to be either overinvestment or malinvestment.
- The *Economist* reported that other developed countries outside of Asia had experienced a similar inflation in housing prices. "The S&P/Case-Shiller national index, the best gauge of American house prices, peaked last year after rising by 134 percent in the previous decade. France, Sweden and Denmark have all had booms of similar size. In Britain, Australia, Spain and Ireland, the ten-year increase … has been even larger."[7] Thus, China's exchange rate policy and its shadow effect in other Asian economies may be contributing to significant distortions in investment decision-making worldwide. Since actual housing prices have risen much faster than housing price models based on the rates of household formation and real income growth would suggest, these increases in housing prices in developed countries outside of Asia may also be bubbles that will eventually burst with similar growth-restraining effects to what the United States is now experiencing.
- During the bubble years, the speculative finance of housing became common. Prudent lending practices such as significant down-payments and the verification of a potential borrower's income, assets, and liabilities were swept aside. Marginal borrowers that might not be able to service their mortgage loans after teaser rates expired relied on ever rising housing prices to allow them to refinance their homes or sell them at a profit before higher rates kicked-in. These subprime residential mortgage loans were securitized into collateral debt obligations (CDOs) and sold to investors that did not understand the credit quality of the underlying loans and that instead relied on the ratings of credit agencies. After the bubble burst, many of these CDOs were unable to perform as their credit ratings implied, and their market value collapsed. Major commercial and investment banks were forced to write down the value of their CDO assets. The revulsion toward CDOs led to a wider re-

evaluation of risk and re-pricing of credit. Despite significant injections of liquidity by the Federal Reserve since September 2007, the availability of credit for riskier transactions such as leveraged buyouts has contracted, and credit risk spreads have widened considerably. From July 2, 2007 to February 15, 2008, for example, the yield spread between Moody's seasoned 20-year grade Aaa (highest investment grade) corporate bonds and comparable Treasuries widened by 60 basis points, while the yield spread between Moody's seasoned 20-year grade Baa (the lowest investment grade) corporate bonds and comparable Treasuries expanded by 91 basis points (see Graph 6). Moreover, the yield spread between the Merrill Lynch index of "junk" corporate bonds (rated CCC by Standard and Poor's) and comparable Treasuries ballooned by 556 basis points. It has become more difficult and more costly for higher risk borrowers to obtain credit. This may reduce aggregate business investment in nonresidential structures, equipment and software and could make a recession more likely.

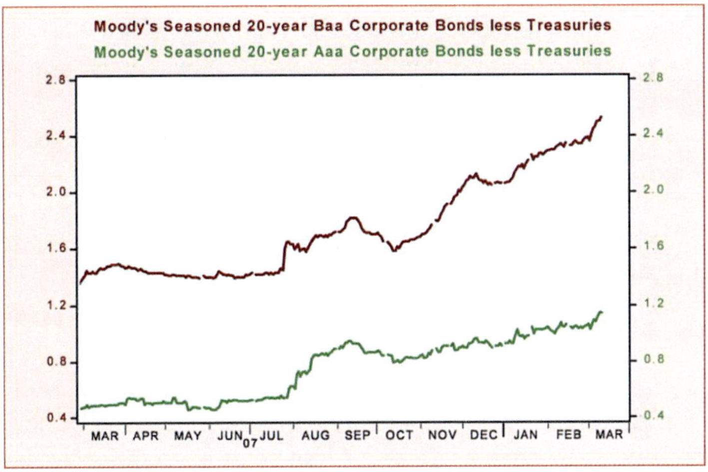

Source: Haver Analytics

Graph 6. Yield Spreads Widened after July 2, 2007

V. DANGERS AHEAD

The present imbalances in exchange rates and international accounts are unlikely to be sustainable.

- The PBC's ability to sterilize its rapidly increasing foreign exchange reserves may have reached its limit. Inflation is accelerating in China. Excess liquidity is inflating prices of assets as well as goods and services. In January 2007, consumer prices were up 7.1 percent from a year ago. Share prices on Chinese stock markets appear to be a bubble. From December 31, 2005 to January 14, 2008, share prices rose by 405 percent as measured by the Dow Jones Shanghai index before backing down by 15 percent through February 15, 2008. Domestic inflation is now affecting China's export sector. After five years of decline, the prices of Chinese manufactured exports are now increasing. The PBC has increased domestic interest rates six times in 2007 and expected to hike domestic interest rates further in 2008. In a desperate measure to curb swelling inflation, the Chinese Banking Regulatory Commission has imposed quotas limiting new loans at Chinese banks.
- Chinese leaders now face a politically uncomfortable choice between (1) maintaining current exchange rate policy to protect the vested interests in the current industrial structure at the cost of spiraling domestic inflation, or (2) allowing a rapid appreciation of the foreign exchange value of the renminbi to a market-determined level to cool domestic inflation and reduce international trade frictions.
- If Chinese leaders decide to allow the foreign exchange value of the renminbi to appreciate to a market-determined level, the dissipation of PBC's massive intervention in foreign exchange may cause the foreign exchange value of the U.S. dollar, which has already been decreasing, to drop further. Decisions by other Asian countries to allow their currencies to appreciate as well would amplify the depreciation of the foreign exchange value of the U.S. dollar.
- The disinflationary effects of the China price in other economies are likely to dissipate over the next few years through either renminbi appreciation or domestic inflation in China. To prevent domestic inflation from accelerating in the United States, the Federal Reserve may need to pursue a less accommodative monetary policy. As a result, long-term interest rates in the United States are likely to be higher.

- A lower foreign exchange value for the U.S. dollar should stimulate the tradable goods and services sector by increasing exports and reducing imports relative to baseline trends. Consequently, both the U.S. current account deficit and the U.S. capital and financial account surplus are likely to fall as a percent of GDP. However, higher long-term interest rates are also likely to prolong declines in housing prices and investment in residential construction and slow the liquidation of overinvestment and malinvestment in housing. Although beneficial to growth over the long term, a reduction in foreign exchange intervention is likely to dampen real GDP growth for several years.
- A major risk for the United States is that Asian central banks and SWFs in oil-exporting countries decide to reduce their exposure to fluctuations in the U.S. dollar by selling U.S. dollar-denominated assets and buying assets denominated in other currencies, probably euros. While some policymakers have hypothesized that the PBC or SWFs might try to liquidate a substantial portion of their U.S. dollar-denominated assets in a political maneuver against the United States, this scenario is highly unlikely because such a "fire sale" would impose enormous financial losses on any country trying to liquidate its U.S. dollar-denominated assets at once. A plausible scenario is that the Asian central banks and SWFs may decide to allocate a smaller share of their portfolios to U.S. dollar-denominated assets over several years. Such a marginal portfolio reallocation could nevertheless place significant downward pressure on the foreign exchange value of the U.S. dollar for an extended period.
- A significant and sustained rally in the foreign exchange value of the U.S. dollar is unlikely to occur until market expectations for the future course of tax, regulatory, and trade policies after the 2008 election improve.

VI. CONCLUSION

The PRC's exchange rate policy and the shadow policies of other Asian governments have boosted the foreign exchange value of the U.S. dollar significantly above its market-determined level since 2000. These policies have distorted price signals around the world by holding down the prices of labor-intensive goods and lowering long-term interest rates. These distortions contributed to unsustainable imbalances in international accounts and to overinvestment and malinvestment, especially in housing in the United States.

If the PRC were to announce its intention to phase-out the PBC's interventions in foreign exchange markets over several years and to allow the renminbi to appreciate more rapidly until its foreign exchange value was determined solely by market forces at some fixed date in the future, the unwinding of these international imbalances and the liquidation of overinvestment and malinvestment would accelerate. Although this policy change would significantly improve the long-term growth prospects for China, the United States, and the rest of the world, it may slow real GDP growth in the United States for several years.

Robert P. O'Quinn
Senior Economist

APPENDIX: WHAT ARE INTERNATIONAL ACCOUNTS?

International accounts are a system of double-entry accounting that records all transactions between residents in a country and nonresidents during a time period, usually a year. In this system, there are two major accounts: (1) **current account** and (2) **capital and financial account**. This is subdivided into: (2a) **capital account** and (2b) **financial account.**

- (1) The current account records transactions in goods, services, income, and unilateral current transfers between residents and nonresidents.
- (2a) The capital account records capital transfers between residents and nonresidents, such as debt forgiveness and migrants' transfers, and acquisitions and disposals of non-produced, non-financial assets between residents and nonresidents.
- (2b) The financial account records transactions between residents and nonresidents resulting in changes in the level of international claims or liabilities, such as in deposits, loans, ownership of portfolio investment securities, and direct investment.

By definition, the (1) current account and the (2) capital and financial account should sum to zero for each country in the world. Thus, a current account surplus implies a capital and financial account deficit and vice versa. Any sum other than zero indicates errors by a country's statistical agency in recording and compiling international transaction data. To compare international account components both among countries and through time, economists normalize balance amounts with a country's contemporaneous gross domestic product (GDP). For example, the U.S. current account balance was 6.15 percent of GDP in 2006.

While many people falsely assume that any surplus must be good and any deficit must be bad, a current account surplus (or a surplus in any of its components including the trade balance) is not necessarily good for a country's economy nor is a current account deficit necessarily bad. Remember, a current account surplus requires a capital and financial account deficit. For example, a country whose economy is in a depression typically runs a current account surplus (because domestic demand for imports has collapsed) and a capital and financial account deficit (because residents and foreigners invest their funds in other countries).

End Notes

[1] In the United States, the dollar is the name of both the currency and the unit of account. In the People's Republic of China, the renminbi is the name of the currency, but yuan is the name of the unit of account. Thus, this study uses renminbi when referring to the Chinese currency as a concept and yuan when referring to an amount in terms of renminbi.

[2] U.S. Treasury debt securities are obligations of the U.S. government that carry the backing of the full faith and credit of the U.S. government. U.S. agency debt securities are obligations of U.S. government agencies or U.S. government-sponsored enterprises (GSEs) that do not carry the explicit backing of the full faith and credit of the U.S. government. However, bond market participants behave as if U.S. agency debt securities carry an implicit guarantee from the U.S. government. GSEs that regularly issue U.S. agency debt securities include the Federal National Mortgage Association (Fannie Mae), the Federal Home Loan Mortgage Corporation (Freddie Mac), and the Student Loan Marketing Association (Sallie Mae). Agencies that regularly issue U.S. agency debt securities include the Federal Farm Credit Banks, the Federal Home Loan Banks, and the Tennessee Valley Authority (TVA). As of December 31, 2007, U.S. Treasury debt securities outstanding were $4.517 trillion and U.S. agency debt securities outstanding were $8.836 trillion.

[3] For a discussion about the international account including definitions of the current account and the capital and financial account, please see the appendix.

[4] Overinvestment is investment that creates more assets than are needed to satisfy current demand for goods and services. Malinvestment is investment that creates the wrong kind of assets to satisfy current demand for goods and services. Overinvestment is generally less costly to liquidate than malinvestment. While overinvestment in assets can be liquidated by reducing new investment in such assets and by lowering the prices of such assets, malinvestment can be liquidated only by adapting existing assets to new uses often through additional investment. Thus, the losses to current asset owners are generally greater from malinvestment than from overinvestment. For example, a home builder may simply suspend new construction on single family detached houses until the inventory clears, while a developer that is constructing a condominium tower in a heavily overbuilt market may have to convert this project to a hotel at considerable expense.

[5] Morris Goldstein, "A (Lack of) Progress Report on China's Exchange Rate Policies," Presented to China Balance Sheet Conference (May 2007). Found at: http://www.chinabalancesheet.org/Documents/ExchangeRate.doc

[6] Gross federal debt is composed of federal debt in intra-governmental accounts and federal debt held by the public. Federal debt held by the public is composed of federal debt held by the Federal Reserve and privately held federal debt. By accounting convention, privately held federal debt includes all U.S. Treasury debt securities owned by international organizations and foreign residents. Foreign residents include foreign governments as well as foreign households and firms. *See Treasury Bulletin,* Table OFS-2 (November 20, 2007). Calculation of percentage is by author.

[7] Economic Focus: House Built on Sand, *Economist* (September 13, 2007). Found at: http://www.economist.com/finance/economicsfocus/displaystory.cfm?story_id=9804125

In: Economic Crises as a Result of Distrust
Editors: Emilio Gullini
ISBN: 978-1-60741-355-4

Chapter 2

FINANCIAL CRISIS: LESSONS FROM CHILE

J.F. Hornbeck

SUMMARY

Chile experienced a banking crisis from 1981-84 that in relative terms had a cost comparable in size to that perhaps facing the United States today. The Chilean Central Bank acted quickly and decisively in three ways to restore faith in the credit markets. It restructured firm and household loans, purchased nonperforming loans temporarily, and facilitated the sale or liquidation of insolvent financial institutions. These three measures increased liquidity in the credit markets and restored the balance sheets of the viable financial institutions. The Central Bank required banks to repurchase the nonperforming loans when provision for their loss could be made and prohibited distribution of profits until they had all been retired. Although the private sector remained engaged throughout the resolution of this crisis, the fiscal costs were, nonetheless, very high.

The U.S. Congress is contemplating a $700 billion government assistance package to arrest the financial crisis in the United States. President Bush argued that failure to enact legislation quickly could result in a wholesale failure of the U.S. financial sector. As discussion of the Administration's plan unfolded, however, questions in Congress arose over issues of magnitude and management of the "bailout," the need for oversight, and the possibility that less costly and perhaps more effective alternatives might be available.

In this light, Chile's response to its 1981-84 systemic banking crisis has been held up as one example. The cost was comparable relative to the size of its economy to that facing the U.S. Government today. In 1985, Central Bank losses to rescue financially distressed financial institutions were estimated to be 7.8% of GDP[1] (equivalent to approximately $1 trillion in the United States today). The policy options Chile chose had similarities as well as differences from those contemplated in the United States today. Their relevance is debatable, but they do highlight an approach that succeeded in eventually stabilizing and returning the Chilean banking sector to health, while keeping the credit markets functioning throughout the crisis.

COMPARING FINANCIAL CRISES

The seeds of the Chilean financial crisis were much different than those in the United States. Nonetheless, in both cases, the financial sector became the primary problem, with policy makers concerned over the prospect of a system-wide collapse. Chile's problems originated from large macroeconomic imbalances, deepening balance of payments problems, dubious domestic policies, and the 1981-82 global recession that ultimately led to financial sector distress. Although most of these are not elements of the U.S. crisis, there are a number of similar threads woven throughout both cases.

Broadly speaking, both countries had adopted a strong laissez-faire orientation to their economies and had gone through a period of financial sector deregulation in the years immediately prior to the crisis. A group of scholars characterized Chile's orientation toward the financial sector as the "radical liberalization of the domestic financial markets" and "the belief in the 'automatic adjustment' mechanism, by which the market was expected to produce a quick adjustment to new recessionary conditions without interference by the authorities."[2]

In both cases, given the backdrop of financial sector deregulation, a number of similar economic events occurred that ultimately led to a financial crisis. First, real interest rates were very low, giving rise to a large expansion of short-term domestic credit. With credit expansion came the rise in debt service, all resting on a shaky assumption that short-term rates would not change. In both cases, but for different reasons, rates did rise, causing households and firms to fall behind in payments and, in many cases, to default on the loans.[3] The provision for loan losses was inadequate causing financial institutions to restrict credit. Soon, many found themselves in financial trouble or insolvent, resulting in the financial crisis. Chile's response may prove useful as policy makers evaluate options.

THE CHILEAN BANKING CRISIS OF 1981-84

Following the coup against socialist President Salvador Allende in 1973, General Augusto Pinochet immediately re-privatized the banking system. Banking regulation and supervision were liberalized. Macroeconomic conditions and loose credit gave way to the economic "euphoria of 1980-81." The exuberance included substantial increases in asset prices (reminiscent of a bubble) and strong wealth effects that led to vastly increased borrowing. The banking system readily encouraged such borrowing, using foreign capital, that because of exchange rate controls and other reasons, provided a negative real interest rate. From 1979 to 1981, the stock of bank credit to businesses and households nearly doubled to 45% of GDP. This trend came to a sudden halt with the 1981-82 global recession.[4]

The financial sector found itself suddenly in a highly compromised position. Weak bank regulations had allowed the financial sector to take on tremendous amounts of debt without adequate capitalization. Debt was not evaluated by risk characteristics. Most debt was commercial loans, but banks also carried some portion of consumer and mortgage debt. As firms and households became increasingly financially stressed, and as asset prices plummeted, the solvency of national banks became questionable. Two issues would later be identified: the ability of borrowers to make debt payments, and more importantly, the reluctance of borrowers to do so given there was a broadly-held assumption that the government would intervene. By November 1981, the first national banks and financial institutions that were subsidiaries of conglomerates failed and had to be taken over by regulatory authorities.[5]

Most debt was short term and banks were in no position to restructure because they had no access to long-term funds. Instead, they rolled over short-term loans, capitalized the interest due, and raised interest rates. This plan was described by one economist as an unsustainable "Ponzi" scheme, and indeed was a critical factor in bringing down many banks as their balance sheets rapidly deteriorated. From 1980 to 1983, past-due loans rose from 1.1% to 8.4% of total loans outstanding. The sense of crisis further deepened because many of the financial institutions were subsidiaries of conglomerates that also had control over large pension funds, which were heavily invested in bank time deposits and bank mortgage bonds. In the end, although the roots of the banking crisis were different than those in the United States, the Chilean government faced the possibility of a complete failure of the financial sector as credit markets contracted.[6]

The Government Response

The Central Bank of Chile took control of the crisis by enacting three major policies intended to maintain liquidity in the financial system, assist borrowers, and strengthen lender balance sheets. These were: 1) debt restructuring for commercial and household borrowers; 2) purchases of nonperforming loans from financial institutions; and 3) the expeditious sale, merger, or liquidation of distressed institutions.[7]

Debt Restructuring

From the outset of the rescue plan, the Chilean Central Bank considered providing relief to both debtors and lenders. There were two rationales. First, as a matter of equity, there was a sense that households as well as firms should be helped. Second, to maintain a functioning credit market, both borrowers and lenders needed to be involved. The Central Bank decided to restructure commercial, consumer, and mortgage loans. The goal was to extend the loan maturities at a "reasonable" interest rate. The debtor was not forgiven the loan, rather banks were given the means to extend the maturities of the loans to keep the debtor repaying and the credit system functioning. Restrictions were in place. Eligible firms had to produce either a good or service, eliminating investment banks that held stock in such firms. Only viable businesses were eligible, forcing the bankruptcy procedures into play where unavoidable. To keep the program going, the loan conditions of each subsequent iteration of the program became easier: longer maturities; lower interest rates; and limited grace periods.[8]

The program allowed Central Banks to lend firms up to 30% of their outstanding debt to the banking system, with the financing arrangement working in one of two ways. At first, the Central Bank issued money, lent it to debtors, which used it to pay back the bank loans. Later, the Central bank issued money to buy long term bonds from the banks, which used the proceeds to restructure the commercial loans. Variations of this process were applied to consumer and mortgage debtors. In cases where loans were made directly from the Central Bank to the debtor, repayment was expected usually beginning 48 months after the loan was made. The fiscal cost was significant, approximating 1% of GDP in 1984 and 1985.[9]

Restoring Bank Balance Sheets

This program was more controversial and had to be adjusted over time to be effective. The key idea was to postpone recognition of loan losses, not forgive them. It relied on identifying nonperforming loans and giving banks time to provision against them, without risking insolvency. The process has been variously characterized as the Central Bank taking on bad debt through loans, purchases, or swaps. All three concepts play some part of this complex, largely accounting-driven arrangement.

Initially, this program was described as a sale, although there was no exchange of assets. The Central Bank technically offered to "buy" nonperforming loans with non- interest bearing, 10-year promissory notes. Banks were required to use future income to provision against these loans and "buy" them back with the repurchase of the promissory notes. In fact, they were prohibited from making dividend payments until they repaid the Central Bank in full. The banks, though, actually kept the loans and administered them, but did not have to account for them on their balance sheets. This arrangement was intended to encourage banks to stop rolling over non-performing loans, recognize the truly bad ones, and eventually retire them from their portfolios. The banks benefitted by remaining solvent and gaining time to rebuild their loan loss reserves so to address nonperforming loans. The credit market was served by banks being able to continue operating with increased funds from released loan-loss reserves.[10]

This program did not work as hoped at first and had to be adjusted. The Central Bank allowed more time for banks to sell nonperforming loans and also permitted a greater portion of their loan portfolios to qualify. It also began to purchase these loans with an interest-bearing promissory note. The banks, however, actually repaid the interest-bearing note at a rate 2 percentage points below that paid by the Central Bank to the banks. This added differential was sufficient incentive for the banks to sell all their bad loans to the Central Bank, beginning a process of identifying good loans and allowing for the eventual retirement of bad loans from the balance sheets (and the banking system). The cost to the Central Bank increased, but by 1985, the portfolio of non-performing loans at the Central Bank began to decline and was eventually eliminated.[11]

Restructuring Distressed Banks

A major goal of government actions was to ensure that bank owners and creditors were not absolved of responsibility to help resolve the crisis, including using their own resources to absorb some of the costs. The government worked closely with all financial institutions to impose new risk-adjusted loan classifications, capital requirements, and provisioning for loan losses, which would be used to repurchase loans sold to the Central Bank. The banks, through the Central Bank purchase of substandard loans, were given time to return to profitability as the primary way to recapitalize, and became part of the systemic solution by continuing to function as part of the credit market.

A number of banks had liabilities that exceeded assets, were undercapitalized, and unprofitable. Their fate was determined based on new standards and they were either allowed to be acquired by other institutions, including foreign banks, or liquidated. The "too big to fail" rule was apparently a consideration in helping keep some institutions solvent. A total of 14 financial institutions were liquidated, 12 during the 198 1-83 period. In most cases, bank creditors were made whole by the government on their deposits with liquidated banks. For three financial institutions that were closed in 1983, depositors had to accept a 30% loss on their assets.[12]

POSSIBLE LESSONS FROM CHILE'S BANK CRISIS

The overriding goal of a strategy to correct systemic crisis in the financial sector is to ensure the continued functioning of credit markets. Chile succeeded in accomplishing this goal and restoring a crisis-ridden banking system to health within four years. The single most important lesson of the Chilean experience was that the Central Bank was able to restore faith in the credit markets by maintaining liquidity and bank capital structures through the extension of household and consumer loan maturities, the temporary purchase of substandard loans from the banks, and the prompt sale and liquidation of insolvent institutions. Substandard loans remained off bank balance sheets until the viable institutions could provision for their loss from future profits. Other losses were covered by the government.

In addition, a number of other insights emerged from the Chilean crisis:

- The market could not resolve a system-wide failure, particularly in the case where there was a high expectation of a government bailout.

- The expectation of a bailout became self-fulfilling and increased the cost.
- Appropriate prudential supervision and regulation were critical for restoring health and confidence to the financial system. Observers lamented the *a priori* lack of attention to proper regulation.
- Private institutions that survived shared in the cost and responsibility to resolve the crisis to the apparent long-term benefit of the financial sector.
- The fiscal cost of the three policies discussed above was high. Liquidating insolvent institutions had the highest cost followed by the purchase of non-performing loans and rescheduling of domestic debts. The strategy, however, is widely recognized as having allowed the financial system and economy to return to a path of stability and longterm growth.

End Notes

[1] Bosworth, Barry P., Rudiger Dornbusch, and Raúl Labán, eds. *The Chilean Economy: Policy Lessons and Challenges*. Washington, D.C. The Brookings Institution. 1994. p. 41.

[2] Ibid., p. 8 and 339.

[3] In the case of Chile, longer maturities were not widely available so debt had to be rolled over regularly. In the United States, various types of adjustable-rate mortgages given to high-risk borrowers eventually led to massive defaults when interest rates and payments ballooned. The financial problem facing U.S. institutions was compounded by the highly complex and arguably poorly understood securitization of these mortgages.

[4] Ibid., p. 38 and Barandiarán, Edgardo and Leonardo Hernández. *Origins and Resolution of a Banking Crisis: Chile 1982-86*. Santiago: Central Bank of Chile. Working Paper No. 57. December 1999. pp. 13-14.

[5] Barandiarán and Hernández, op. cit., pp. 20-22.

[6] Ibid., pp. 15-18 and 21-23 and Bosworth, Dornbusch, and Labán, op. cit., p. 339.

[7] Barandiarán and Hernández, op. cit., p. 20-23. In addition, because a portion of the debt in Chile was dollar denominated, the government created a preferential exchange rate program to help repay those debts, the value of which had balooned on the balance sheets of corporate and household debtors because of the 1982 peso devaluation. Because this issue is not germane to the U.S. situation, it is not further discussed. The preferential exchange program nonetheless represented a large subsidy that the government of Chile had to absorb.

[8] Ibid., pp. 25-29.

[9] Ibid., pp. 25-26. There was also a cost in expanding the money supply, but the macroeconomic effects proved limited and are not addressed here.

[10] Ibid., pp. 29-30 and Bosworth, Dornbusch, and Labán, op. cit., pp. 41 and 340.

[11] Ibid.

[12] Barandiarán and Hernández, op. cit., pp. 40-46 and Bosworth, Dornbusch, and Labán, op. cit., p. 402.

In: Economic Crises as a Result of Distrust
Editors: Emilio Gullini
ISBN: 978-1-60741-355-4

Chapter 3

FINANCIAL CRISIS: LESSONS FROM SWEDEN

James K. Jackson

SUMMARY

In the early 1990s, Sweden faced a banking and exchange rate crisis that led it to rescue banks that had experienced large losses on their balance sheets and that threatened a collapse of the banking system. Some analysts and others argue that Sweden's experience could provide useful lessons for the execution and implementation of the Emergency Economic Stabilization Act of 2008[1]. The banking crisis facing the United States is unique, so there are no exact parallels from which to draw templates. Sweden's experience, however, represents a case study in how a systemicbankingcrisis was resolved in a developed country with democratic institutions. The Swedish central bank separated out good assets, which it left to the banks to oversee from bad assets, which it placed in a separate agency with broad authority to work out debt problems or to liquidate assets. Four lessons that emerged form Sweden's experience are: 1) the process must be transparent; 2) the resolution agency must be politically and financially independent; 3) market discipline must be maintained; and 4) there must be a plan to jump-start credit flows in the financial system. This chapter provides an overview of the Swedish banking crisis and an explanation of the measures Sweden used to restore its banking system to health.

Background

Sweden's banking crisis grew slowly over time and was the result of a number of policy decisions[2]. In particular, the crisis arose from a set of economic policies that attempted to: 1) support Sweden's fixed exchange rate policy, 2) deregulate the financial sector, 3) expand credit, and 4) provide low-cost loans for residential purchases and for university students. Eventually, a drop in asset values weakened the balance sheets of banks and reduced liquidity in the economy. One key factor in Sweden's financial crisis was a set of policy measures the country adopted in the mid-1980s to liberalize the highly regulated financial sector. Prior to this liberalization, banks, insurance companies, and other institutions were subjected to lending ceilings and were required to invest in bonds issued by the government and mortgage institutions.

Large central government deficits and a national policy that favored residential investment led to requirements that banks hold more than 50% of their assets in such bonds, typically with long maturities and low interest rates. In addition, the banks were carefully scrutinized and monitored by Riksbank, Sweden's central bank. This close supervision meant, however, that the banks themselves were unaccustomed to performing risk analysis, and were ill-prepared to perform risk analysis on commercial paper associated with real estate loans. This lack of experience led to unhealthy risk taking when the nation began to deregulate its financial sector and allow banks to participate in a broader array of financial instruments. Indeed, some analysts argue that it was this inexperience, rather than the deregulation effort itself, that played a role in the banking crisis. Sweden also favored housing and college education by operating a system that provided loans with highly favorable terms with little or no credit evaluation. Other economic problems compounded Sweden's efforts to gain control over the macroeconomic conditions within the country and place the economy on a well-balanced positive growth track[3].

Deregulation

In the early to mid-1980s, Sweden began deregulating its financial markets at such a rapid pace that it took most observers by surprise[4]. In part the deregulation was spurred by the rapid development that had occurred in the growth of money market accounts, certificates of deposit, and government securities that arose from growing central government budget deficits. These actions shifted Sweden's monetary policy to an expansive posture and allowed banks, mortgage institutions, finance companies, and others to compete in the domestic credit market. The expansion in credit helped stimulate economic growth, but it also fed inflation and added to general expectations of inflation in the economy. In addition, Sweden's tax system stimulated consumer borrowing by allowing taxpayers to fully deduct interest payments and exchange controls stimulated corporate borrowing by favoring domestic investment over foreign investment.

These activities combined with an expansionary fiscal policy to increase credit in the economy added to the stock, or the overall amount, of debt. This credit boom pushed up the prices of corporate stocks and real estate — both commercial real estate and residential housing. As the pace of economic growth accelerated, the rate of price inflation also increased, which led to the Swedish Krona being overvalued. By the late 1980s, Sweden removed a broad range of foreign exchange controls, but it maintained its fixed exchange rate system. During this time, Sweden experienced current account deficits and large outflows of direct investment and other long-term capital, which led to a growing stock of private sector short-term debt in foreign currency[5]. In essence, Swedish households and businesses were borrowing in foreign currency at interest rates that were below those that were charged for loans denominated in Swedish Krona. The result of this borrowing was a substantial amount of exchange rate risk in the balance sheets of the private sector.

By the early 1990s, a combination of reforms in the tax system and periods of high interest rates caused asset prices to fall. As the pace of economic growth cooled, the rate of unemployment began to rise, public sector debt rose, bankruptcies surged, and the banking system was shocked as the rising bankruptcies forced banks to curtail their lending activities in order to build up their loan loss reserves. A further setback for the economy occurred with German reunification in 1990, which resulted in higher German interest rates and an appreciating currency. Sweden's fixed exchange rate policy obligated Sweden to import the higher German interest rates, pushing its own interest rates higher and busting a property market bubble. When Sweden was forced to abandon its exchange rate peg in November 1992, the real exchange rate fell substantially, while real interest rates remained high, which caused a large number of private sector loans to become non-performing.

THE FINANCIAL CRISIS

In early 1990, Sweden's economy appeared to be doing well. The unemployment rate was at an all-time low and the stock market was booming. At the same time, the rate of price inflation was rising, the real effective exchange rate was appreciating, and there was a general consensus that the economy was growing at an unsustainable rate. In addition, rising stock market prices reinforced the continued expansion in real estate, especially in the commercial property market. By mid-1990, however, commercial occupancy rates had fallen, pushing down the price of stocks for both the real estate and construction sectors[6].

The first financial firm to feel the effects of the drop in real estate prices was Nyckeln, one of Sweden's fastest growing financial firms. Nyckeln, like other financial firms, was owned by several of Sweden's largest banks. Nyckeln had achieved its rapid growth by specializing in commercial real estate financing and financing its operations through a new type of commercial paper called *marknadsbevis*, which the banks had guaranteed. At this time, Sweden's commercial paper market had become the third largest commercial paper market in Europe. In 1991, the value of commercial paper dropped sharply when interest rates in Sweden began rising as a result of rising international rates that were pushed up by German reunification. With the fall of Nyckeln, two of Sweden's six largest banks were heavily affected and announced that they could not meet their regulatory capital requirements.

Concern quickly spread through all of Sweden's commercial paper market, which essentially shut down. By the end of the year, three of Sweden's major financial firms had defaulted. Two of the major banks faced actual insolvency problems and the government of Sweden, the major shareholder in the two banks, injected equity into one of the banks and issued guarantees to the other bank for loans that enabled the banks to fulfill their capital requirements. By the spring of 1992, yet another Swedish bank went bankrupt. At this point, the Swedish government took ownership of the third bank and began to treat the defaults and bankruptcy as a crisis. The government refused to offer complete forbearance of the non-performing loans and did not offer unlimited liquidity support, but opted to guarantee the bank's debts, an action it would extend to all of Sweden's banks within a few weeks.

As a major step in resolving the banking crisis, the central bank divided each bank into two separate entities, one with its good assets, the other with its bad assets. The entities holding the good assets continued to operate under their old names and were later merged under a new name. The bad assets were transferred to two asset management companies. The asset management companies were owned by the government, but had a high degree of independence and were free of many of the regulations that applied to banks. The management companies attempted to assess the value of the non-performing loans they had inherited and then moved to rescue whatever economic value they could. As a result, the companies injected equityinto troubled borrowers to maintain and restore their values and, at times, took over defaulting companies, which they ran as a private owner until the companies could be liquidated. Assets were sold in three ways: initial public offerings on the Stockholm stock exchange; corporate transaction outside the stock exchange; and transactions involving individual properties. A quick rebound in the Swedish economy that stemmed from an increase in economic growth in Europe and elsewhere allowed all of the managed assets to be liquidated by 1997, ultimately at a lower cost to the Swedish taxpayers than had initially been projected.

LESSONS LEARNED FROM SWEDEN'S EXPERIENCE

Each financial crisis is unique and largely dependent on the specific combination of national and international factors that exist at the time. In addition, the resolution of the crisis is intricately interwoven with a broad set of laws and national characteristics that are unique to each crisis and each national setting. A number of differences between the Swedish and U.S. experiences are readily apparent.

- Unlike the situation in the United States, the Swedish government had a financial stake in the largest banks prior to the crisis. This made the Swedish government a direct stakeholder in the institutions and provided an impetus for it to act.
- Sweden's real estate loans and commercial paper were nearly all domestically held, so that it did not face both a domestic and international financial issue.
- Many nonperforming loans in Sweden were a result of unhedged private sector exchange rate risk when the currency peg collapsed.
- In the United States, the financial sector problems are linked to the securitization of mortgages, which led to credit exposures that extended well beyond the retail banking sector.
- Sweden's economy is small and open, which enables it to rely on an export-led recovery strategy. The U.S. economy is larger relative to the global economy and it has a strong influence on the pace of global

economic growth. As a result, the United States is more likely to rely on a recovery strategy that is based on domestic demand.

An analysis of the Swedish banking crisis of the 1990s reveals that there are a number of factors that were inherently responsible for the resolution of the crisis that apply specifically to the Swedish case. Despite these caveats, the Swedish experience may offer some insight into one possible way of resolving a domestic financial crisis. One factor that helped Sweden quickly resolve its financial crisis was a strong international economic recovery that pushed up real estate values in Sweden and improved the balance sheets of banks. Others argue that a number of procedural factors, in addition to the economic recovery, helped bring the financial crisis to a resolution. In particular, they argue that four factors played an important role in this process in Sweden and could prove beneficial in resolving other financial crises:[7]

- First, transparency of the process is important. In Sweden, expected losses were recognized early on and helped to preserve the confidence of the market.
- Second, the process seems to work best with a politically and financially independent agency. This type of structure shields decision makers from political pressures, especially as banks are closed and assets are liquidated. Financial independence of the agency gives credibility to the notion of political independence. In addition, financial independence allows for a rapid response when funding needs emerge suddenly and waiting for a government appropriation is impractical.
- Third, is the importance of maintenance of market discipline and avoiding blanket guarantees. According to this concept, extending blanket guarantees increases the risk of future financial crisis because it weakens market discipline exerted by uninsured creditors. Blanket guarantees of all the liabilities of problem institutions in the throes of a crisis reduces the credibility of claims that such guarantees will not be extended in future bank failures. Although the guarantees were intended to calm the markets, some analysts argue they likely reduced incentives to monitor bank risk by creditors. Some analysts argue that a better solution would be a bank holiday that would allow bank examiners enough time to assess the extent of non-performing loans while it would allow insured depositors access to their funds. In addition, uninsured depositors would be allowed to move their funds out, but would be forced to assume some of the losses. Also non-viable banks would not be

eligible to receive financial support from the government and public funds would not be used to support a non-viable institution.

- Fourth, is a plan to jump-start credit flows in the financial system by repairing the damaged creditworthiness of the broader economy. Even if banks can be completely restored to financial health through recapitalization, borrowers may be in no position to repay any new loans they may get. Such a plan may include such items as a fiscal stimulus to aid borrowers.

End Notes

[1] Dougherty, Carter, Stopping a Financial Crisis, The Swedish Way, *The New York Times*, September 23, 2008; Purvis, Andrew, Sweden's Model Approach to Financial Disaster, *Time*, September 24, 2008.

[2] Englund, Peter, The Swedish Banking Crisis: Roots and Consequences, *Oxford Review of Economic Policy,* Autumn 1999. P. 80-97.

[3] Ibid, p. 83-84.

[4] Ingves, Stefan, *The Nordic Banking Crisis From an International Perspective*, International Monetary Fund, September 11, 2002.

[5] Backstrom, Urban, *What Lessons Can be Learned From Recent Financial Crises? The Swedish Experience.* Federal Reserve Symposium "Maintaining Financial Stability in a global Economy," August 29, 1997.

[6] Englund, The Swedish Banking Crisis, p. 84-89.

[7] Ergungor, O. Emre, *On the Resolution of Financial Crises: The Swedish Experience*, Federal Reserve Bank of Cleveland Policy Discussion Paper, June 2007, p. 1-12.

In: Economic Crises as a Result of Distrust
Editors: Emilio Gullini
ISBN: 978-1-60741-355-4

Chapter 4

FINANCIAL MARKET TURMOIL AND U.S. MACROECONOMIC PERFORMANCE

Craig K. Elwell

SUMMARY

A large and relatively unimpeded flow of credit through healthy financial markets is a salient attribute of the U.S. economy and any well functioning modern economy. Banks and other financial institutions channel the economy's savings toward a variety of current productive uses. By borrowing short-term and lending long-term, these institutions create a flow of credit that passes liquidity from savers to investors, and transforms liquid short-run assets into less liquid long-term assets. These long-term assets are created by credit-financed, current spending by households on housing, consumer durables, and education, and by, current spending by businesses on new plant and equipment. But lending in credit markets requires confidence in the borrowers' ability to repay the debt (principal and interest) in full and on schedule. The current turmoil in U.S. financial markets is the result of a breakdown in that necessary confidence. In an environment of distrust, financial institutions are far less willing and able to lend long-term. The move toward short-term lending diminishes the flow of long-term credit to the non-financial economy and dampens the economic activities of households and businesses that are dependent on borrowing. Economic policy may be needed to get credit flowing smoothly again and to mitigate the damage incurred by households and non-financial businesses. A number of indicators have pointed to a substantial rise in the cost of credit and a decrease in the flow of credit to the broader economy.

A reduced flow of credit will likely dampen economic activity that is dependent on such borrowing as residential investment spending (purchasing new homes) by households, business investment spending (purchasing new plant and equipment) and consumer spending (purchasing autos, appliances, and higher education) by households. Residential investment spending has fallen over 40% between the fourth quarter of 2005 and the third quarter of 2008, and has on average subtracted about 1.0 percentage point from real GDP growth in each of those six quarters. Non-residential investment spending continued to increase in 2007 and the first half of 2008, but the pace fell steadily, and in the third quarter of 2008 it declined 0.1%. Consumption expenditures had been increasing, but at a decelerating rate in 2007 and the first half of 2008. However, in the third quarter of 2008 consumer spending fell 3.1%. A recent study estimates that the decrement to the U.S. economy's supply of credit is about $1 trillion, leading to a potential drag on real GDP of about 1.8 percentage points for two years.

There are three types of policy response, applied separately or in combination as the severity of the problem warrants. The first type is the conventional macroeconomic policy tools of monetary and fiscal policy, used with the aim of broadly supporting bank liquidity and aggregate spending. Monetary policy, having greater flexibility than fiscal policy, will usually play the prominent role. The second type of policy for responding to a credit crisis is the Fed's traditional role of "lender of last resort," typically involving some expanded use of the Fed's discount window, the facility the Fed uses to make short term loans to banks that need to bridge a short-run shortage of liquidity. These policies will be more narrowly focused on the needs of troubled institutions. The third type of policy response is the use of "extraordinary measures" involving direct interventions by the federal government to restore confidence in financial markets, forcing credit to flow broadly and at greater volume.

INTRODUCTION

A large and relatively unimpeded flow of credit through healthy financial markets is a salient attribute of the U.S. economy and any well functioning modern economy. Banks and other financial institutions channel the economy's savings toward a variety of current productive uses. By borrowing short-term and lending long-term, financial institutions create a flow of credit that passes liquidity from savers to investors and which transforms liquid short-run assets into less liquid long-term assets.

These long-term assets are created by credit financed current spending by households on housing, consumer durables, and education; and current spending by businesses on new plants and equipment. In a highly developed financial system, this flow of credit will not only be to households and non-financial businesses, but also to other financial institutions to meet occasional short-term needs for liquidity that serves to minimize disruptions in the flow of credit to the non-financial economy.

This act of borrowing short-term and lending long-term, however, makes financial institutions less liquid and therefore inherently vulnerable to crisis. It is a sustainable situation, however, so long as there is widespread confidence, particularly among lending institutions themselves, in the quality of the assets being created. Specifically, it requires confidence in the ability of those assets to sustain a flow of earnings sufficient, at a minimum, to meet the lending institutions' short-term borrowing costs (liabilities).

The current turmoil in U.S. financial markets is the result of a breakdown in that necessary confidence. In an environment of distrust, financial institutions are less willing or able to lend long-term. While still willing to borrow short-term, in the face of great uncertainty they will tend to also lend short-term in an attempt to enhance their own liquidity. They prefer to hold riskless Treasury securities that offer almost no return rather than lend to a business or consumer who presents even moderate risk. The move toward short-term lending diminishes the flow of long-term credit to the non-financial economy and dampens the economic activities of households and businesses that are dependent on borrowing.

The breakdown of confidence in U.S. financial markets is an outgrowth of the end of the housing boom in 2006 and the subsequent fall of home prices. As home prices fell sharply in many areas of the country, a surge in delinquencies and foreclosures on mortgage loans occurred, reducing the flow of earnings to lenders who held these nonperforming mortgages. As the fall in earnings grew larger, it became increasingly evident by the late summer of 2007 that an unusually high percentage of the mortgages and mortgage backed securities (MBSs) created during the housing boom were of lower quality then originally estimated. The initial overvaluing of these assets has been attributed to an adverse interaction between lax underwriting practices by the originators of the loans and deficient evaluations by credit rating companies of the MBSs created with those loans. These shortcomings were easily overlooked so long as home prices were rising, but became evident once home prices fell.

The fall in the value of these mortgages and mortgage related assets translated into growing losses for the financial institutions who held them. As their balance sheets deteriorated, so did their ability to lend to each other and to lend to the non-financial economy. The financial market disruptions escalated during 2008. Because of the wide distribution and complex structure of many MBSs it became very difficult for a potential lender to confidently appraise the quality of assets on the balance sheet of potential borrowers and the risk of the borrower defaulting on the loan. Thus even well capitalized banks became reluctant to lend. As research by psychologists has shown, fear of loss is often a stronger motivator than the prospect of gain, explaining why in a crisis, financial institutions' concern for preserving wealth overrides the desire to increase wealth.

The rational choice for any one burdened financial institution is to reduce its debt by selling assets. But, as many similarly burdened institutions attempt to reduce debt by simultaneously selling assets, the price of assets is driven sharply down, deteriorating their balance sheets further rather than improving them. The constriction of the flow of credit is accordingly magnified and that, in turn, increases the drag on economic activity in the credit dependent non-financial sectors.

Left to market forces alone, this systemic failure would arguably only resolve it self slowly and at great cost to the wider economy. The Great Depression is seen by many economists as an example of the perils of leaving the resolution of a major financial crisis to the markets themselves. Recent research shows that "fire sales" driven by a sharp increase in investors preference for liquidity can push asset prices below their fair market value and be very costly to the financial system by forcing the inefficient liquidation of long-term investments and to the wider economy by reducing the availability of credit for productive endeavors.[1]

Therefore, mainstream economists today argue that economic policy measures are needed to get credit flowing smoothly again and to mitigate the damage incurred by households and non-financial businesses. The form and scope of such policy initiatives can, nevertheless, vary. Further, because of the substantial interdependence of the global financial system, a coordinated policy response by the affected countries could be needed.[2]

EVIDENCE OF TIGHTER CREDIT CONDITIONS

A number of indicators have pointed to a substantial rise in the cost of credit and a decrease in the flow of credit to the non-financial sectors of the U.S. economy. These include

- Despite the Fed's lowering the federal funds rate by 4.25 percentage points between September 2007 and October 2008, the added liquidity did not cause most mortgage interest rates to ease. The rates on non-conforming jumbo loans have risen substantially.
- Despite the Fed's efforts to bolster the inter-bank loan market, the growing turmoil has caused the so-called TED spread, the difference between what banks and the Treasury pay to borrow money to rise to exceptional heights. Usually this spread would be 50-70 basis points, by October 2008 it soared to 464 basis points.[3] Such a large spread suggests a huge increase in perceived risk and a great reluctance of banks to make short-term loans to each other.
- According to the Fed's July and September 2008 surveys of senior loan officers for a sample of banks, most banks are tightening lending standards for residential mortgages, consumer loans, and business loans. The change of standards were decreased loan size, decreased loan term, increased level of collateral required, and an increased spread of the loan rate above the banks' cost of funds.
- New issues of speculative grade bonds have fallen and the interest rate on lower grade corporate bonds has increased.
- Credit extended by banks has fallen from about $1.1 trillion in the fourth quarter of 2007 to only $211 billion in the second quarter of 2008.[4]

Credit flows will reflect the interaction of supply and demand in financial markets. All of the above indicators of tighter credit conditions have emerged at a time when economic activity, for reasons separate from events in financial markets, has been slowing, an event that would weaken the demand for credit and otherwise tend to loosen credit conditions. This configuration of economic forces suggests that it is a diminished supply of credit that is causing the tightening of credit conditions in U.S. financial markets.

THE EFFECT OF TIGHTER CREDIT CONDITIONS ON MACROECONOMIC ACTIVITY

Financial markets exert their influence on real economic activity by affecting both the price and the quantity of credit supplied to borrowers in the non-financial sectors of the economy. It is expected that a higher price of credit (higher interest rates) will dampen credit supported spending by households and businesses. It is perhaps less obvious that changes in the quantity of credit offered (credit rationing) to non-financial borrowers can have an effect on their spending apart from the effect of increased price. In a financial crisis, banks and other lending institutions can become so illiquid or risk averse that even at higher interest rates, little credit will be made available to long-term borrowers—and a true credit crunch emerges.

A reduced flow of credit will tend to dampen economic activity highly dependent on borrowing, such as residential investment spending (purchasing new homes) by households, business investment spending (purchasing new plant and equipment) and consumer spending (purchases of autos, appliances, and higher education) by households.

In a situation where the prices of assets owned by households are falling, there are likely to be two primary channels of negative effect on consumer spending: the direct dampening effect of tighter credit conditions, and the indirect dampening effect on spending caused by a decrease in household wealth due to declining prices of homes and of financial assets held by consumers.

Slower spending by households and businesses slows the growth of real GDP, the most general measure of overall economic well-being and a possible precursor of rising unemployment.

U.S. aggregate economic activity has been slowing for some time. In 2006, real GDP increased 2.8%, a pace generally considered close to the economy's sustainable long-term rate of growth. In 2007, the pace of real growth slowed to 2.0%, as the weakness of the housing sector became a significant drag on economic activity. More deceleration has occurred during 2008, with an outright decline of real GDP of 0.5% in the third quarter. (The third quarter GDP number is a preliminary estimate and subject to revision.)

Much of the economic weakening in 2008 is attributable to a sizable loss in real purchasing power caused by sharply higher energy and food prices, which has slowed several categories of aggregate spending. But it is also possible that the further weakening of economic activity in the third quarter of 2008 reflects the added dampening effects of the turmoil in financial markets beginning to spread to the broader economy. If so, such negative effects would likely be evident in the most credit-sensitive categories of aggregate spending.

Impact of Tight Credit on Residential Investment

So far, the effect of progressively tighter credit conditions in 2007 and 2008 has been most evident on real residential spending, which is highly sensitive to changes in the price and quantity of mortgage lending. The inventory of unsold homes was reported to be around 4.5 million units or equivalent to about an eleven month supply.[5] Similarly, housing starts have fallen precipitously from over 2 million units in 2006 to an annual rate of about 800 thousand units through September 2008, or a total decline in housing starts of about 60%.[6]

In terms of GDP growth, real residential investment spending has fallen over 40% between the fourth quarter of 2005 and the third quarter of 2008, and on average has subtracted about 1.0 percentage points from real GDP growth in each of those six quarters. Because residential investment spending typically accounts for only about 5% to 6% of GDP in normal circumstances, economic weakness in the housing sector by it self may slow the economy but is unlikely to cause it to stall if other spending categories remain strong.[7]

A significant factor in the sizable decrease of residential investment has likely been a sharp slowing of the flow of mortgage credit from lenders. As recently as the fourth quarter of 2007, mortgage lending to households occurred at an annual rate of $635 billion, but that flow had diminished to $81 billion by July 2008.[8]

The recovery of residential investment spending will likely require a recovery of the flow of mortgage credit. However, even if there is a relatively quick improvement in credit conditions, the large inventory of unsold homes suggests that residential investment will continue to be a drag on the economy well into 2009.

Impact of Tight Credit on Business Investment

Real non-residential investment spending continued to increase in 2007 and the first half of 2008 despite the growing turmoil in U.S. financial markets. Since then, the rate of increase has been slowing. After advancing 7.5% in 2006, the pace of spending by businesses on new plant and equipment slowed to 5.0% in 2007, and through the second quarter of 2008 that pace had slowed to about 2.3%. In the third quarter of 2008, however, real nonresidential investment declined 0.1%.[9]

It is likely that a recent history of substantial profits reduced the need for corporations to use external sources of funds to finance investment spending. That insulation has so far allowed this category of spending to largely avoid the dampening effect of deteriorating credit conditions.

However, over the four quarters ending in June 2008, non-financial corporate profits advanced only 0.8%. In a slowing economy, a further weakening of profit performance can be expected. This prospect makes it unlikely that businesses can continue to use internal funds to finance such a large share of investment spending. The fall of real nonresidential investment in the third quarter of 2008, although small, suggests to some that for many businesses a point as been reached where a dwindling flow of credit becomes a significant constraint on non-residential investment spending. For most corporations the primary credit constraint is not likely to be a lack of bank credit but the inability to issue bonds on affordable terms.

Beyond the cost of borrowing, businesses' willingness to undertake investment spending will be strongly influenced by their expectation of the future demand for their products. In anticipation of meeting strong demand in the future, businesses increase current investment spending to add production capacity needed to meet future demand. If, on the other hand, there is an anticipation of weak demand, businesses are likely to reduce their current investment spending. That expectation will be contingent on the expected spending by consumers. A sizable slowing of consumer spending is likely to deteriorate businesses' expectations of future consumer spending, inducing a slowing of non-residential business investment.

Impact of Tight Credit on Consumer Spending

Consumer spending is the largest component of GDP, accounting for about 70% of total aggregate spending. In addition, consumer spending tends to be relatively stable, generally free of wide swings and decreasing in only the most severe economic downturns. Nevertheless, given its great size, even modest swings in consumption spending will have a strong influence on the growth of GDP through both its direct effect and its indirect effect on business investment spending. As discussed above, business investment spending will slow if the expectation for the growth of demand for their products is downgraded following signs of slower consumer spending.

Real consumption expenditures had been increasing, but steadily decelerating their rate of advance in 2007 and the first half of 2008. After increasing about 3.0% in 2006, that pace slowed to 2% in 2007, and through the first half of 2008 slowed further to about a 1% annual rate.

However, in the third quarter of 2008, real consumer spending fell sharply, down 3.1%.[10] That's large enough to subtract 2.25 percentage points from the growth rate of real GDP in the third quarter and could indicate that the economy is in the midst of a sizable down turn. The deceleration of consumer spending over the past year is substantially the result of lost purchasing power due to the sharp rise in energy and food prices. Only in the third quarter of 2008 has there been mounting evidence of tight credit conditions dampening consumer spending.

Until recently, the flow of credit to households (other than mortgage lending) was not greatly diminished. As recently as the fourth quarter of 2007, bank loans to households increased at an annual rate of nearly $63 billion. By the second quarter of 2008, however, bank loans to households *decreased* at a $52 billion annual rate. This diminished flow of bank credit could constrain many types of consumer purchases such as autos, major appliances and higher education.

In contrast, the flow of consumer credit (largely credit cards) has remained relatively strong through the second quarter of 2008, down from an annual pace of $136 billion in 2007 but still increasing at a $114 billion annual rate in the second quarter of 2008. This pattern of borrowing probably indicates that households have been running up their credit card balances to sustain their spending. If so, consumer spending may weaken further, since such a pattern of spending cannot be sustained indefinitely.

The effect of tighter credit on consumer spending is likely to be more evident in the sub-category of consumer durable goods. These are expenditures that are typically financed by borrowing and are also purchases that can be postponed until economic conditions improve. Real consumer durable spending began to decline in late 2007, decreasing 4.3% and 2.8% in the first two quarters of 2008 respectively. The third quarter spending drop was much greater, down 14.1%, resulting in a 1 percentage point decrement from the third quarter's real GDP growth rate.

The biggest contributor to the decline of consumer durable goods purchases is a sharp fall in automobile sales in 2008, down from about 16 million units in 2007 to an annual rate of less than 13 million units over nine months of 2008. In addition to tighter credit conditions, record high gasoline prices likely contributed to the weak automobile sales over the whole period, as has the steady fall in household wealth caused by falling home prices (see next section's discussion of this effect). Nevertheless, the sharpness of the third quarter fall is also probably a manifestation of the abrupt further deterioration of credit conditions that occurred around mid-year.

The Effect on Consumer Spending of Falling Asset Values Reducing Household Wealth

In addition to the direct dampening effect of tighter credit conditions on consumer spending, there is likely to be an indirect dampening effect caused by falling asset prices reducing household wealth. Falling prices for stocks and bonds decreases the value of households' retirement and investment portfolios, inducing consumers to spend less and save more in an attempt to replenish lost wealth. In addition, falling home prices erase accumulated equity, decreasing a ready source of liquidity for households to finance current expenditures. Also tighter credit conditions and tougher loan terms may make it more difficult to convert any remaining wealth (equity) into liquidity (cash).

Economic research indicates that for every $100 billion decrease in household wealth, consumer spending tends to fall $4 billion to $10 billion, with the change emerging over a one- to two-year period.[11] Over the last year, household net worth declined nearly $3 trillion. If past relationships continue to hold, that decrease in wealth could cause a cumulative decrease in consumer spending of between $120 billion and $300 billion. A spending change of that size would translate into a drag on economic growth equivalent to 1.0% to 2.5% of GDP. That spending reduction could grow larger if home and other asset prices continue to fall, causing household wealth to continue to fall.

The Double-Edged Influence of the International Sector on GDP

International Flows of Goods

In addition to relatively steady consumer spending, the U.S. economy's ability to maintain moderate real GDP growth over the last two years, despite the sharp fall of the housing sector and unprecedented disruptions in financial markets, is largely explained by the strong growth of real net exports since mid-2006.

The strength of net exports has been a consequence of relatively stronger economic growth among major U.S. trading partners and of more competitively priced American goods resulting from the over 30% decline in the dollar's real (trade-weighted) exchange rate from 2002 through 2007.

In 2007, real export sales increased 8.4% while import purchases increased only 2.2%. Through the first half of 2008, export sales have remained strong and import purchases have actually decreased. This pattern was strongly evident in the second quarter of 2008, when net exports generated nearly all of that quarter's annualized GDP growth rate of 2.8%. In the third quarter, real export sales fell off their second quarter pace, but were still strong, and imports continued to decline. Overall, net exports contributed 1.1 percentage points to the third quarter's real GNP growth, continuing as a source of economic strength, but not strong enough to offset the quarter's sharp fall in consumer spending.[12]

Whether this pattern of strong net export growth can continue is open to question. The pace of economic growth in foreign economies is slowing due to a combination of reduced purchasing power caused by high energy and food prices, credit constraints as a result of the spread of the negative effects of the U.S. credit crisis to many industrial economies with closely linked financial markets, and less accommodative policy responses by foreign governments. The prospect of slower economic growth abroad is likely to weaken the demand for U.S. exports and reduce their positive impulse on real growth in the United States over the near term.

International Flows of Capital (Assets)

The depreciation of the dollar since 2002 has been animated by a slow but steady weakening of the demand for dollar-denominated assets on the part of foreign investors, reducing the inflow of foreign capital. This gradual ebbing of the foreign inflow of capital is equivalent to a reduction in the inflow of foreign credit (lending), but it has not over this period been disruptive or caused any abrupt increase in U.S. interest rates. Nevertheless, capital outflows are likely to have a heightened significance in the current state of financial turmoil and diminished credit flows to the domestic economy.

The negative effect on domestic credit conditions would be more substantial if the inflow of capital slows sharply. That could happen if foreign investors, faced with the financial turmoil in the United States, suddenly decide that dollar assets are too risky. An abrupt fall in capital inflows would be an added decrement to the supply of credit, exerting stronger upward pressure on U.S. interest rates, exacerbating the negative effects already affecting the credit and interest rate sensitive sectors of the economy.

For the 12 months through June 2008, the U.S. Treasury reports that the U.S. economy received a net foreign inflow of foreign capital of $270 billion, down from $879 billion during the preceding twelve months. This overall inflow was largely sustained by official purchases (inflows of capital from foreign central banks), more than offsetting net outflows of capital by foreign private investors. However, in July 2008 there was a net capital outflow of $75 billion, reflecting the joint effect of a net outflow of $92 billion by private investors and a net inflow of $18 billion from other foreign central banks.[13]

If this pattern of large reductions of foreign capital inflows continues along with a weakening demand for U.S. exports, the near-term negative effects of this capital outflow on credit sensitive economic activity risk offsetting any concurrent positive effects from net exports.

If, however, economic conditions abroad deteriorate greatly, a "flight to quality" towards dollar assets, particularly low-risk Treasury securities, may have a positive effect on credit conditions in the United States. The recent strength of the dollar suggests that this move into highly liquid dollar assets is occurring, but it is an open question whether it will be sustained.

An Estimate of the Potential Drag on Real GDP Growth from a Diminished Flow of Credit

Although the GDP data indicate that the economy has weakened in 2008, it is difficult to say how much of the slowdown evident so far is attributable to the ebbing of credit flows to the nonfinancial sectors. The sharp surge in energy and other commodity prices are thought to have had a significant dampening effect on economic activity in 2008, and there were clear signs that the economy was already slowing prior to the recent escalation of financial turmoil, in part due to the weakness of residential investment since 2006, and in part due to the erosion of real purchasing power caused by increased energy prices. It is likely that the negative effects of 2008's financial market turmoil on the real economy will be partially evident in the second half of 2008 and more fully evident in 2009. How big an economic blow might be coming?

A Simulation of the Effect of a Diminished Credit Flow on Real GDP

A recent study contains an estimate of the potential overall effect of reduced credit flows on real GDP.[14] It examines the linkage running from home prices falling, to mortgage credit losses and reduced capitalization of leveraged financial institutions, to a reduced supply of credit flowing to households and non-financial business. This study is not presented as the last word on this subject, but it is carefully constructed and presents plausible estimates of gross magnitudes of effect and has the added advantage of being timely.

The study focuses on the supply of credit provided by three sets of financial institutions: (1) on balance-sheet lending by banks (and other leveraged financial institutions), (2) off-balance sheet lending by the asset backed securities (ABS) market, and (3) lending by government-sponsored enterprises (GSEs). The study estimates the dampening effect of the reduced flow of credit from these three sources on the rate of growth of real GDP.

The central projection of the study is based on the assumption that home prices fall 10% from their mid-2008 level. Mortgage credit losses are projected to accumulate to $636 billion through 2012. Given a series of assumptions about tax rates, recapitalization rates, and leverage ratios, a credit loss of that size is projected to cause a decrement to the U.S. economy's supply of credit of about $1 trillion, and lead to a drag on real GDP of about 1.8 percentage points for two years. For an economy that is likely already growing significantly below its trend rate of near 3%, this degree of drag from deteriorating credit flows has the potential to halt real economic growth over the next two years.

A particularly critical assumption for this outcome is that Fannie Mae and Freddie Mac (the main GSEs) continue to expand credit growth at their recent pace. Over the past year, despite a decline in the market value of their equity capital, the GSEs have accelerated their contribution to credit growth, adding almost $620 billion of lending over the year ending in June 2008. The study's central projection of credit growth has the GSEs continuing to expand their lending at a $750 billion annual rate. (This outcome is more plausible now that the GSEs are controlled by the government.)

However, if the GSEs should stop expanding their lending, the study estimates that the decrement to total credit growth would increase to $1.7 trillion, and the estimated drag on real GDP would increase to 3.2 percentage points over the next two years. That would be a substantial blow to overall economic activity and probably, other factors constant, has the potential to generate a deep recession.

These estimates do not include other negative effects of the housing downturn on overall economic activity, such as the wealth related dampening of consumer spending, nor does it reflect the sizable real income losses stemming from higher energy prices. Nevertheless, the study suggests that a substantial credit crunch by itself has the potential to deliver a major negative blow to the economy, potentially inflicting significant economic damage well beyond the housing sector and the financial markets.

Economic Policy Responses to the Credit Crisis

How can economic policy contain or mitigate the potentially large negative economy-wide effects of a major credit crisis? In general, there are three types of policy response to be applied separately or in combination as the severity of the problem warrants. The first type comprises the conventional macroeconomic policy tools of monetary and fiscal policy, used with the aim of broadly supporting bank liquidity and aggregate spending. Monetary policy, having greater flexibility and precision than fiscal policy, will usually cause it to play the prominent role.

The second type of policy for responding to a credit crisis is greater use of the Fed's traditional role of "lender of last resort." This policy will typically involve expanded use of the Fed's discount window, the facility the Fed uses to make short term loans to banks that need to bridge a short-run shortage of liquidity. Theses policies will be more narrowly focused on the needs of troubled institutions and deal more directly with un-blocking the flow of credit than would conventional macroeconomic policy.

The third type of policy response is the use of "extraordinary measures" involving direct interventions by the federal government to restore confidence in financial markets and the remove impediments to credit to flowing broadly and at greater volume. This "extraordinary intervention" may involve a restructuring of the debt of troubled financial institutions and significant changes in the regulation of financial markets. It is also argued that, to be effective, a government most often will need to apply "extraordinary measures" *quickly and decisively* so that the actions clearly remove all uncertainty about profit and loss in the financial sector.

The U.S. government, to date, has employed all three types of policy responses to the current credit market crisis.

Conventional Macroeconomic Policy

Monetary Policy

Monetary policy is the Fed's standard and most frequently used tool to exert broad-based influence on credit conditions and economic activity so as to achieve full employment and price stability. U.S. monetary policy is implemented by targeting (raising or lowering) the short-term federal funds rate, a market-determined interest rate that banks charge each other for short-term loans. The targeting of the federal funds rate is accomplished with open market operations whereby the Fed buys or sells Treasury securities for cash to increase or decrease liquidity in the financial markets, increase or decrease real borrowing costs, and thereby increase or decrease investment (and other credit sensitive) spending.[15]

From the standpoint of financial institutions, open market operations affect the prices of assets and the cost of carrying debt. Through both of those changes, the Fed may be able to influence banks' willingness and ability to lend.

In response to a financial crisis, the Fed would apply a stimulative monetary policy. A stimulative monetary policy is initiated with the Fed entering the federal funds market, making open-market purchases of Treasury securities from banks in exchange for cash. The infusion of cash increases the reserves (liquidity) of the banking system, exerting downward pressure on interest rates. The effect on interest rates is likely to be reflected quickly and most fully on short-term interest rates and then, hopefully, spread to longer-term interest rates. Beginning in September 2007, in response to continuing evidence that "disruptions in financial markets" could have adverse effects on the wider economy, the Fed aggressively applied successive injections of monetary stimulus, as it added reserves and pushed down the federal funds rate from 5.25% to its current level of 1.0%.[16]

However, the stimulative effects of a much lower federal funds rate to the wider economy seem to be substantially muted as evidenced by the failure of long-term interest rates to fall. This lack of a stimulative effect is occurring because banks, still lacking the needed degree of "confidence" have been content to increase reserves and liquidity, but not increase their lending activity. They are still not willing to borrow short-term and lend long-term, the behavior needed to keep an adequate flow of credit (liquidity) moving to the non-financial sectors.

The phrase often used to describe this lack of effect on real economic activity is that monetary policy can not get "traction." In the economic literature, the extreme form of this phenomenon is called a "liquidity trap," a situation where the financial system's seemingly limitless appetite for short-term liquidity keeps the economy stuck in a sub-optimal equilibrium of slow economic growth that monetary policy (alone) cannot push it out of. At this extreme, monetary policy's attempt to move the economy is likened to "pushing on a string."

In the current situation, the economy may not have fallen into a "liquidity trap," and getting the economy back to its trend rate of growth may only be a matter of applying more monetary stimulus. But there may be some restrictions on the Fed's ability to apply more stimulus. For one, the federal funds rate is approaching the "zero bound." When the short-term policy rate is at or near zero, the conventional approach for conducting a stimulative monetary policy is not possible.

However, there are alternative means that the Fed could employ to provide stimulus in this situation. First, the Fed could try to *change financial market's interest rate expectations*. The current interest rate on long-term assets depends on the entire expected future path of short-term interest rates, including the zero rate for the federal funds rate. If the central bank can persuade the public that it will hold the short-term rate at zero for longer than had been expected, interest rates across the whole term-structure should also fall, stimulating spending. Such an outcome would hinge on whether the Fed's policy commitments are taken as credible by the public.

Second, the Fed could *alter the composition of its balance sheet*. The Fed's asset holdings are primarily of Treasury securities of different maturities ranging from one month to 30 years, but because its targeted interest rate for the conduct of monetary policy has been the short-term federal funds rate it has relatively large holdings of short-term securities. (The average maturity of its assets is typically around one year.) If the Fed were to shift the composition of its balance sheet toward long-term assets by selling short-term treasuries and buying long-term treasuries, it could possibly lower long-term yields to provide stimulus to economic activity.[17]

A third option for implementing monetary policy at the "zero bound" is to *expand the size of the Fed's balance sheet*. This, of course, is the conventional means of conducting a stimulative monetary policy of buying securities to increase the supply of reserves in the banking system. The policy focus, however, is shifted from the price of reserves (interest rates) to the quantity of reserves. This process of increasing reserves above the level consistent with keeping the policy interest rate at zero was used by Japan during its financial crisis of the 1990s and is often called "quantitative easing."[18]

Stimulative monetary policy at the zero bound was the major part of Japan's initial response to its financial crisis in the 1990s. That policy, for the reasons just discussed, had a very difficult time getting "traction" and was not by itself able to push the Japanese economy out of crisis.

Nevertheless, operation of monetary policy at the zero bound for the federal funds rate would be a passage through uncharted waters for U.S. monetary policy. There remains substantial uncertainty about how well the alternative operating procedures might work, particularly given the important role often volatile investor expectations would play in the alternative procedure's ability to stimulate economic activity.

Another important constraint on the Fed's ability to conduct a stimulative monetary policy is the risk of inflation. After 2006, inflation began to accelerate. The Consumer Price Index (CPI) increased 2.5% in 2006, but through July 2008 the CPI was rising at about a 5.4% rate. Much of the upward pressure on the price level was the consequence was a sharp rise in energy and other commodity prices. In addition, the falling dollar had increased the domestic price of many imports.

In August and September of 2008, inflation slowed substantially, perhaps indicating that economic growth has slowed enough to remove much of the upward pressure on energy and food prices. If so, this apparent abatement of supply-side generated inflation may allow the Fed to worry less about near term inflation effects of a large scale monetary stimulus to counter the dampening effect on economic activity of the current financial market crisis.

There is still the issue of long-term inflation effects of current monetary stimulus. The Fed has injected large amounts of liquidity into the economy that could pose an inflation problem once the economy returns to a normal rate of growth. However, measures of inflation expectations have fallen since June 2008.[19]

Nevertheless, policies in addition to monetary stimulus were thought to be needed to get credit flowing and support aggregate spending.

Fiscal Policy

Fiscal policy can support economic growth through an increase in the budget deficit via lower taxes and increased government spending (including both changes in discretionary spending and changes in the automatic stabilizers). A policy of fiscal stimulus would involve tax cuts or spending increases (or some combination of the two). Unlike monetary policy, which must transmit its stimulative impact to economic activity indirectly through financial markets, fiscal policy has a relatively direct impact on economic activity. Increased government spending is a direct addition to aggregate spending. A tax cut is less direct because it must first pass through household income before it boosts spending, and there is always the possibility that all or part of the tax cut is saved rather than spent by households. In addition to its effect on aggregate spending, fiscal stimulus may have an indirect positive effect on the condition of financial institutions' balance sheets as the salutary effect on economic activity also exerts upward pressure on asset prices[20]. To be most effective, fiscal policy initiatives would occur in conjunction with a stimulative monetary policy.

The Economic Stimulus Act of 2008[21] provided tax rebates to households and accelerated depreciation rules for business that amounted to an increase in private sector income of about $120 billion in 2008.[22] Taking potential multiplier effects into consideration, the rebate could generate an even larger stimulus to total economic activity.[23] History and economic theory, however, indicate that one-time tax cuts often do not stimulate consumer spending. Nevertheless, evidence from the 2001 federal tax rebate showed that households eventually spent about 2/3 of that rebate. The Bureau of Economic Analysis's estimate of personal saving increased substantially in the second and third quarters of 2008, suggesting that a substantial portion of the 2008 rebate has been saved so far.[24]

In addition, the "automatic stabilizers," which are policies or programs designed to provide an offset to current economic trends without additional legislation, have been enhanced by extending the term of unemployment benefits from 20 weeks to 40 weeks. Because unemployment benefits tend to get spent quickly, they usually give a timely and direct stimulus to economic activity.[25]

Total real federal spending over the four quarters ending mid-2008 has increased about 5%, and contributed an estimated 0.4% to the growth of real GDP over this period.[26] However, to correctly gauge government's effect on aggregate spending, its revenue and spending actions need to be evaluated. The generally accepted way of determining whether the influence of the government budget on aggregate spending and real GDP is positive or negative is the direction of change of the "standardized budget measure."

The standardized measure excludes the effect of cyclical fluctuations and factors that are short- lived and unlikely to affect aggregate spending in the shortrun. The Congressional Budget Office (CBO) projected in October that the standardized budget deficit increased from 1.1% of potential GDP in 2007 to 2.8% of potential GDP in 2008, which suggests that government fiscal actions are expected to provide a stimulative impulse to the economy equal to 1.7% of potential GDP. In 2009, however, the standard budget deficit is projected to fall to 1.6% of potential GDP, which signals a reduction of the government budget's stimulative effect on aggregate spending. (This estimate pre-dates legislation that is discussed below that provides a major increase in government expenditures for rescue of the financial system.)[27]

The Fed as "Lender of Last Resort"

In the role of "lender of last resort," the Fed offers credit to solvent but temporarily illiquid financial institutions. These are financial institutions that are solvent because the value of their assets exceed the value of their liabilities, but because their debts tend to be short-term and liquid while their assets are long-term and illiquid, they are in need of short-term funds to meet short- term debt obligations. The expectation is that with improved access to short-term liquidity, financial institutions will be more willing and able to lend to each other and to the non-financial sectors of the economy, and thereby remove excess volatility in financial markets.

The Fed's "discount window" is its facility for making loans to financial institutions with short- term liquidity problems and the "discount rate" is the interest rate charged for these loans.[28] Financial institutions are often reluctant to use the discount window out of concern that financial market participants will draw a negative inference about their financial condition if their borrowing from the Fed becomes known. In conjunction with conventional monetary stimulus (discussed above), the Fed, beginning in August 2007, has taken a number of steps to make use of the discount window more attractive. It has broadened the group of eligible participants, it has extended the term of loans, and it has lowered the discount rate.

Enhancements to the Fed's lender of last resort function have included the creation of the Primary Dealer Credit Facility which opened the discount window to non-member financial institutions, the Term Auction Facility to make loans to member banks based on a broader range of collateral, and the Term Securities Lending Facility to lend Treasury securities in exchange for some asset backed securities. The Fed has also entered into asset swaps with the European Central Bank and several other foreign central banks to increase dollar liquidity in foreign financial markets. (These direct loans to the financial sector are typically "sterilized" by the Fed through the purchase of Treasury securities so as to keep the total value of its asset holdings steady and avoid generating any inflationary pressure.)

Maintaining market confidence in the financial sector also involves ensuring that any exit of firms from the sector occurs in an orderly way. To this end, the Fed in March 2008 facilitated with loans the purchase of a troubled investment bank, Bear Stearns, by J.P. Morgan. The Fed judged that, given the severe illiquidity of the financial system at that time, a bankruptcy filing by Bear Stearns would have led to much broader liquidity problems. The Fed argued that lending support for the sale of Bear Stearns was necessary to avoid the systemic risk of a disorderly exit.

The Fed's enhanced discount window initiatives have pumped a large volume of liquidity into the U.S. financial system. For the two month period ending October 1, 2008, the Fed increased system-wide reserve funds by over $800 billion, increasing total reserve funds to over $1.5 trillion. For comparison, reserve funds increased only about $27 billion over the twelve months ending June 2008.[29]

Despite their size, the Fed's lender-of-last-resort initiatives (along with conventional monetary stimulus) have not yet resulted in renewed credit flows at pre-crisis levels, as financial institutions have accumulated reserves, but remained reluctant to generate new long-term lending. This lack of effect has suggested to some that the problem goes beyond a matter of short-run illiquidity, and involves long-term solvency issues. (Long-term insolvency means that the "true" market value of some financial institutions' assets is not sufficient cover their liabilities.)

The Fed's ability to continue pursuing large "lender-of-last-resort" activities may eventually be constrained by the changing risk profile of the central bank's balance-sheet. Its recent "lender of last resort" initiatives have meant that the Fed has exchanged a sizeable portion of its holdings of low-risk Treasury securities for high-risk collateral. Although the Fed is able to hedge some of this risk, the average level of risk carried in the Fed's total asset holdings has increased. More lending by the Fed could potentially increase the level of risk in its asset holdings to a point beyond which it is not willing to go.

Extraordinary Measures (Large Scale Intervention)

The Fed has implemented extensive "lender of last resort" measures to help the financial sector bridge temporary liquidity problems of turning assets into cash and avoiding selling at "fire-sale" prices. The Fed has also continued to apply a stimulative monetary policy that has provided liquidity, lowered market interest rates at the short end of the yield curve, and increased the demand for financial assets. The objective of both policy initiatives is to reduce the risk of insolvency and assuage banks' reluctance to lend long-term.

The "conventional initiatives" alone were not seen to be enough, however. In two bold steps beyond the conventional, the government, to forestall bankruptcies that could be particularly devastating to the whole financial system, took control of the mortgage giants Fannie Mae and Freddie Mac and the insurance giant AIG.

Nevertheless, despite these efforts, the financial turmoil persisted, credit flows remained anemic, risk spreads remained at record size, and the threat of more widespread bankruptcies of financial institutions increased. The prospect of a collapse of the entire financial system, with large negative repercussions on the wider economy, prompted the federal government to initiate a massive intervention into the financial system to restore confidence and resume the flow of credit. Hence, the Troubled Asset Relief Program (TARP) was initiated with a variety of features, but the heart of the program is that it gives the Secretary of the Treasury up to $700 billion to either buy mortgages and other troubled assets or directly recapitalize selected financial institutions.[30]

How Will TARP Work?

The details of how the program will be fully implemented are still being developed. A central objective, however, is to increase demand relative to supply for risky assets in order to stabilize their price. Arguably, the government will now target, as it does the federal funds rate, the price of risk in the economy. Stabilizing the price of risk may reduce the incentive of financial institutions to hoard liquidity and induce them to return to their conventional role of borrowing short-term and lending long-term, and begin to pass a larger flow of liquidity to the non-financial sectors to support credit dependent spending.

In general, there are at least two ways for TARP to stop the price of risky assets from falling. First, the Treasury can reduce the supply of risky assets by buying them or guaranteeing them (a guarantee reduces the supply because it transforms a risky asset into a not risky asset). Second, the Treasury can recapitalize the financial system either through inducing it to capitalize itself or through the government taking some level of equity position in troubled financial institutions. With recapitalization, the demand for risky assets is expected to recover, exerting upward pressure on asset prices. (The initial spending of TARP funds has been for recapitalization.)

Within this general framework, critical decisions, therefore, must be made about *what assets* to buy or guarantee: whole mortgages and mortgage pools; mortgage backed securities; or "other assets" deemed important to promote financial market stability. In addition, decisions will be made about *what price* to pay for the troubled assets. The Treasury could either buy at "market price," to protect taxpayers, or it could buy at "above market price," to provide recapitalization of the assisted institution, conferring a significant benefit to that institution but none to many others.

Will TARP Solve the Problem?

TARP takes the U.S. economy into uncharted waters and it is uniquely difficult to predict what the outcome of the program will be. Many economists argue that some initiative broadly like this was probably needed to stave off an economic catastrophe that would have extended far beyond the housing sector and Wall Street. One lesson that some have drawn from Japan's banking troubles in the 1990s was the Japanese government's failure to act quickly and decisively in restructuring financial sector debt was an important reason why Japan emerged from its financial crisis so slowly, enduring a decade of lost economic growth.

If such a large and extraordinary intervention into U.S. financial markets is needed to assure their smooth functioning, it raises the longer term question of whether the management of risk can largely be left to financial markets themselves. Some argue that permanent public guarantee of risk could be necessary to avoid overly volatile asset markets, to ensure the ability to issue debt, and to preserve an adequate flow of credit to the non-financial economy.

Sceptics counter that large scale government support and guarantee of risk may induce "moral hazard"; that is, if financial markets come to believe that government will come to the rescue any time problems occur, then those markets will have less incentive to prudently manage risk and more incentive to take on imprudent risk. To resolve the moral hazard problem posed by TARP, more extensive prudential supervision and regulation of financial markets may be required.

FORECASTING THE U.S. ECONOMY'S PATH THROUGH THE FINANCIAL CRISIS

Economic forecasts are different from simulation studies such as the one above. A forecast of the rate of growth of real GDP attempts to incorporate all of the significant forces, positive and negative, that are likely to influence economic growth. Among these forces are the expected effects of current and anticipated economic policy initiatives to counter the negative effects of the financial crisis. Nevertheless, some perspective on the expected magnitude of the repercussions on economic activity can be gained from how economic forecasts have changed over the year as the financial turmoil has unfolded.

Most forecasts at the beginning of 2008 projected some slowing of economic growth due to the effects of the housing crisis, rising energy prices, and conventional cyclical forces. The degree of the financial market melt-down that emerged in the spring was not anticipated in those early forecasts, however, and would force sizable revisions of most forecasts by the fall. Focusing on 2009, the first full year when the economic repercussions on economic growth would be most evident, the following revisions have occurred:

- The IMF's October 2008 forecast for U.S. real GDP growth for 2009 has decreased from 1.8% in January 2008 to 0.1%.[31]
- The Congressional Budget Office forecast for growth of real GDP in 2009 has fallen from 2.8% in January 2008 to 1.1% in September 2008.[32]

- The Blue Chip Indicators consensus forecast of U.S. real GDP growth in 2009 has moved down from 2.9% in January 2008 to 2.1% in September 2008.[33]

These forecasts, reflecting the stabilizing and stimulative economic policies in place through September 2008, show the U.S. economy slowing substantially more in the coming year then had been expected before the intensification of the turmoil in financial markets that emerged as 2008 progressed.

Economic forecasts carry a high degree of uncertainty, and most of the risks in the current economic situation are judged to be on the down-side. One important risk is that the constraint on credit flows from the de-leveraging of financial institutions could be deeper and more protracted than expected. A second substantial risk is that the housing prices do not stabilize, and instead deteriorate further. In addition, the global dimension of the crisis broadens the problems beyond the U.S. market and adds the risk of destabilizing shifts in international capital flows.

On the up-side, U.S. economic policy has shown the ability to change quickly and substantially in response to the financial market turmoil, and the United States has a strong record of successfully managing recoveries from business cycle downturns.

End Notes

[1] Franklin Allen and Douglas Gale, *Understanding Financial Crises*, (Oxford: Oxford University Press, 2007).

[2] For background on financial instability and its implications see, Irving Fisher, "The Debt-Deflation Theory of Great Depressions", *Econometrica 1: 1933,* pp 337-357, Charles Kindleberger, Manias, Crashes, and Panics, (New York: Basic Books, 1978), and Hyman Minsky, *Stabilizing an Unstable Economy* (New Haven: Yale University Press, 1986).

[3] Data for the TED spread came from http://www.bloomberg.com/quote?ticker=.TEDSP%3AIND.

[4] Credit flow data came from the Federal Reserve Board, *Flow of Funds Account of the United States, Statistical Release Z.1*, September 18, 2008, Table F.1, at http://www.federalreserve.gov/releases/z1/current/z1.pdf.

[5] National Association of Realtors, "Existing Home Sales," http://www.realtor.org/research/research/ehsdata.

[6] Housing start data reported by U.S. Department of Commerce, Bureau of the Census, New Residential Construction Statistics, November 19, 2008, http://www.census.gov/const/newconstruction.pdf.

[7] The source for GDP data is the U.S. Department of Commerce, Bureau of Economic Analysis (BEA), *U.S Economic Accounts*, http://www.bea.gov.

[8] See Federal Reserve Z.1 data.

[9] See BEA *U.S. Economic Accounts*.

[10] See BEA, *U.S. Economic Accounts*.

[11] See Christopher D. Carol, Misuzu Otsuka, and Jirka Slacalek, "How Large is the Housing Wealth Effect? A New Approach," *NBER Working Paper No. 12746* (Cambridge, MA: National Bureau of Economic Research, December 2006).

[12] See BEA, *U.S. Economic Accounts*.

[13] U.S. Department of the Treasury, Office of International Affairs, Treasury International Capital (TIC) data for August 2008, released October 16, 2008, http://www.treas.gov/press/releases/hp1215.htm.

[14] Jan Hatzius, "Beyond Leveraged Losses: The Balance Sheet Effects of the Home Price Downturn," *Brookings Papers on Economic Activity*, fall 2008, http://www.brookings.edu/economics/bpea/~/media/Files/Programs/ES/BPEA/ 2008_fall_bpea_papers/2008_fall_bpea_hatzius.pdf.

[15] See CRS Report RL34427, *Financial Turmoil: Federal Reserve Policy Responses*, by Marc Labonte.

[16] See the minutes of The Fed's Open Market Committee from September 2007 through October 2008 at[http://www.federalreserve.gov/monetarypolicy/fomc.htm].

[17] For this process to work, however, investors must treat Treasury securities of different maturities as imperfect substitutes, otherwise an increase in the supply of short-term securities coupled with a like-size decrease in the supply of long-term in public hands would not cause a significant decrease in long-term interest rates. The evidence is limited, but it would tend to indicate that the public sees only a small degree of imperfect substitutability between short-term and long-term Treasury securities, raising doubt about the efficacy of altering the composition of the Fed's balance sheet to generate a stimulative monetary policy.

[18] Quantitative easing is thought to affect real economic activity through three channels. First, it induces a shift in investor portfolios away from cash and toward other financial assets, so it would tend to push up asset prices and push down yields. Second, by altering investor expectations about the future path of the federal funds rate by demonstrating a willingness to keep reserves high, it could (as already discussed above) induce a decrease in interest rates. Third, quantitative easing could generate a stimulative fiscal effect as the swapping of non-interest bearing currency and reserves for interest bearing Treasury debt leads to a reduction of the current and future interest cost of the federal government and a lowering of the associated tax burden on the public.

[19] University of Michigan Inflation Expectation, Survey Research Center: University of Michigan, data available at http://research.stlouisfed.org/fred2/series/MICH/.

[20] For further discussion see, CRS Report RS21 136, *Government Spending or Tax Reduction: Which Might Add More Stimulus to the Economy?*, by Marc Labonte.

[21] P.L. 110-185, 122 Stat. 613-622.

[22] For further discussion see, CRS Report RS22850, *Tax Provisions of the Economic Stimulus Package*, by Jane G. Gravelle.

[23] Multiplier effects are the additional increases in aggregate spending that occur when an expansionary fiscal policy increases consumer spending.

[24] See BEA, *U.S. Economic Accounts*.

[25] For further discussion see, CRS Report 92-939, *Countercyclical Job Creation Programs*, by Linda Levine.

[26] See BEA, *U.S. Economic Accounts*.

[27] Congressional Budget Office, *The Cyclically Adjusted and Standardized Budget Measures,* October 2008, http://www.cbo.gov/ftdocs/97xx/doc9768/10-03-StandBudget.pdf.

[28] For further discussion of Fed policy see, CRS Report RL34427, *Financial Turmoil: Federal Reserve Policy Responses*, by Marc Labonte.

[29] Data on reserve growth comes from the Board of Governors of the Federal Reserve System, "Factors Affecting Reserve Balances of Depository Institutions", H.4.1 release, September 25, 2008, http://www.federalreserve.gov/ releases/.

[30] For further discussion, see CRS Report RS22963, *Financial Market Intervention*, by Edward V. Murphy and Baird Webel.

[31] International Monetary Fund, *World Economic Outlook*, October 2008, p. 2, http://www.imf.org/external/pubs/ft/ weo/2008/index.htm.

[32] Congressional Budget Office, "CBO's Economic Projections for Calendar Years 2009-2011", http://www.cbo.gov/ budget/econproj.

[33] Blue Chip forecast can be found in CRS Report RL30329, *Current Economic Conditions and Selected Forecasts*, by Gail E. Makinen, pp. 9-10.

In: Economic Crises as a Result of Distrust
Editors: Emilio Gullini
ISBN: 978-1-60741-355-4

Chapter 5

FINANCIAL MELTDOWN AND POLICY RESPONSE

Jim Saxton

INTRODUCTION

During the week of September 13-20, 2008, the United States confronted the worst global financial crisis in almost a century. Credit markets, which are the circulatory system of the U.S. economy, seized up. The Federal Reserve was unable to revive credit markets through massive liquidity injections. Share prices plummeted, and a run began on money market mutual funds.

Federal Reserve Chairman Ben Bernanke and Secretary of the Treasury Henry Paulson determined that the *ad hoc* approach that the federal government had been taking to resolve this crisis was not working. Instead, the federal government needed a comprehensive plan that would resolve the uncertainty about value of impaired mortgage- related financial assets and the solvency of financial institutions holding these assets.

Secretary Paulson asked Congress to authorize the Treasury to purchase and liquidate up to $700 billion of impaired financial assets from financial institutions. Both credit and equity markets had a favorable initial response, but the subsequent reaction was less positive.

Underlying Causes

The primary cause for this global financial crisis was the popping of the U.S. housing bubble in the second quarter of 2006 and the subsequent steep decline in U.S. housing prices. Falling housing prices revealed speculative excesses and unsound lending practices in housing markets. During the bubble years, the federal government encouraged depository institutions and mortgage bankers through various affordable housing and community reinvestment regulations to extend subprime residential mortgage loans to low income families. Investment banks securitized these subprime mortgage loans into subprime residential mortgage-backed securities (RMBS) and subprime collateralized mortgage obligations (CMOs). Investment banks sold subprime RMBS and tranches of subprime CMOs to financial institutions around the world. After the U.S. bubble popped, many subprime borrowers could not refinance their existing loans. Default and foreclosure rates on these subprime mortgage loans skyrocketed.

Falling housing prices also revealed the vulnerabilities of the alternative financial system based on securitization and highly leveraged non- depository financial institutions (such as Fannie Mae, Freddie Mac, and independent investment banks) that had developed over the last three decade. This alternative to the bank-centric financial system performed the same economically vital, but inherently risky functions of intermediation and liquidity and maturity transformation traditionally performed by commercial banks and other depository institutions. These vulnerabilities, which were the lack of adequate capital standards, the lack of a lender of last resort, and opaque structured credit products, were the secondary cause of this crisis.

A number of mistaken government policies and misaligned private incentives helped to inflate the U.S. housing bubble and contributed to vulnerabilities of the alternative financial system. Two previous Republican JEC studies[1] documented these policy mistakes and private incentive factors in detail.

Independence is an Unsustainable Business Model for Investment Banks

The business model of major investment banks as independent institutions is an artificial construct of the legal separation of commercial and investment banking in the *Banking Act of 1933* (often referred to the *Glass-Steagall Act*) that proved unsustainable after financial services deregulation in an adverse economic environment. This is another example of how well intentioned government regulations often distort economic decision-making and produce structurally weak financial institutions that cannot survive outside of a highly regulated environment and favorable economic conditions.

Universal banking (i.e., the provision of both commercial and investment banking functions within the same financial services firm) is the surviving business model. Of the five major investment banks on Wall Street at the beginning of 2008, none remain as independent entities.

During the last three decades, financial services deregulation increased competition and eroded the excess profits that independent investment banks had traditionally earned from brokerage services and the underwriting of debt and equity securities. To increase fee income, independent investment banks began to underwrite increasingly complex structured credit products, including subprime RMBS and CMOs.

Independent investment banks also sought to increase their spread income (i.e., the difference between the income from financial assets in proprietary portfolios and the interest expense on borrowed funds). From the early 1990s through 2007, independent investment banks funded a large increase in the size of their proprietary portfolios through short-term debt (i.e., repurchase agreements, commercial paper, and secured and unsecured lines of credit with commercial banks).

To achieve the high returns on equity to which independent investment banks were accustomed, the leverage ratios at independent investment banks ballooned relative to the average leverage ratio at commercial banks and saving institutions. At the end of the first quarter in 2008, the leverage ratios at Morgan Stanley, Lehman Brothers, Merrill Lynch, and Goldman Sachs were 31.8, 30.7, 27.5, and 26.9, respectively, compared with an average of 8.8 for all U.S. commercial banks and savings institutions.

Once the global financial crisis began on August 9, 2007, both commercial banks and investment banks incurred significant credit losses on subprime residential mortgage loans and write-downs on subprime RMBS and tranches of CMOs. Commercial banks were better able to absorb these credit losses and write-downs than independent investment banks because commercial banks had significantly higher capital and loss reserve ratios than independent investment banks.

During the first nine months of the global financial crisis, financial firms were able to raise new equity capital to absorb most of their credit losses and write-downs. However, sovereign wealth funds and private investors became increasingly unwilling to invest additional equity capital as share prices declined. The market has forced a general deleveraging and fire sales of financial assets that have been especially stressful for independent investment banks. As the leverage ratios at independent investment banks declined, the returns on equity at independent investment banks fell, and the ability to attract new investments in the equity of independent investment banks diminished.

The rapid expansion of capital and employment in the financial services industry during the boom years of the high-tech stock and real estate bubbles has ended, and a contraction is underway. The exit of independent investment banks from the market through acquisitions or bankruptcies will facilitate the necessary contraction in capital and employment in the financial services industry before a recovery can begin.

FAIR VALUE ACCOUNTING

Fair value accounting (also known as mark-to-market accounting), which was adopted after the bankruptcy of Enron in 2002, exaggerated the real losses that financial institutions had incurred on their portfolios of subprime RMBS and CMOs when these institutions made their quarterly financial reports. Fair value accounting requires financial institutions to use econometric models to estimate the market value of illiquid financial assets (referred to as level three assets) based on various price inputs.

When a distressed financial institution sells one of these illiquid financial assets under stressful market condition, this "fire sale" price establishes a new fair value for similar assets even if a non-distressed seller could obtain a significantly higher price under normal market conditions. Under fair value accounting, financial institutions have made significantly larger write-downs of the subprime RMBS and CMOs on their balance sheets than the actual losses that these financial institutions are likely to incur if they were to hold these assets to maturity or sell them under normal market conditions.

Fair value accounting has created a vicious cycle once the global financial crisis began on August 9, 2007. Based on "fire sale" prices, financial institutions have written down the reported value of their subprime RMBS and CMOs. These reported losses eroded their capital and reduced their share prices. In response, financial institutions curtailed credit to some customers, increased their reserves, sought additional equity, and conducted additional "fire sales" that triggered further industry-wide write-downs, new losses, still lower share prices, credit contractions, and the need for additional equity and reserves.

Intervention Principles

Prior to the announcement of Friday September 19, 2008, Chairman Bernanke and Secretary Paulson had intervened in credit markets during the current crisis based on the principles that economist Walter Bagehot had outlined for central bank behavior during crises more than a century ago.[2] These include:

1. Lend freely to illiquid, but solvent financial institutions based on collateral that would be good under normal market conditions;
2. Charge a penalty interest rate to encourage these institutions to return to private funding sources as soon as possible; and
3. Minimize market disruptions from the liquidation of insolvent financial institutions.

Additionally, Secretary Paulson has tried to minimize the moral hazard risk problems that may arise from federal interventions. At a minimum, Paulson has insisted on:

1. Removal of the Board of Directors and replacement of the CEO; and
2. Substantial dilution of existing common and preferred shareholders through warrants (i.e., the right to buy newly issued shares at fixed price in the future) so that most of any future appreciation in the market value of these firms will go to the taxpayers.

Fannie Mae and Freddie Mac

In July 2008, Secretary Paulson asked Morgan Stanley to conduct an independent review of the financial condition of Fannie Mae and Freddie Mac. Morgan Stanley found each of these government-sponsored enterprises (GSEs) would need a capital infusion of at least $50 billion over the next eighteen months in order to continue their operations.

During August 2008, Federal Reserve and Treasury officials learned that foreign central banks and sovereign wealth funds were reluctant to rollover their large portfolios of GSE debt securities unless both Fannie Mae and Freddie Mac received large capital infusions. On August 26, 2008, Freddie Mac's then CEO Richard Syron reported to Secretary Paulson that Freddie Mac's last-ditch effort to raise capital had failed. Chairman Bernanke, Secretary Paulson, and Federal Housing Finance Agency (FHFA) Director James Lockhart concluded neither GSE would be able to raise the necessary capital. That day, Secretary Paulson discussed the situation with President Bush, and the decision was made to place both GSEs under conservatorships.

On September 7, 2008, Director Lockhart announced that the FHFA had placed both Fannie Mae and Freddie Mac under conservatorships. These conservatorships will continue indefinitely until the FHFA Director determines that these GSEs can operate in a "safe and sound" manner.

1. The FHFA assumed effective control of both GSEs, removing the Boards of Directors and replacing both CEOs. The retired CEO of TIAA-CREF Herbert Allison replaced Daniel Mudd as the CEO of Fannie Mae, and the former CFO of US Bancorp David Moffett replaced Richard Syron as the CEO of Freddie Mac.
2. Each GSE may continue securitizing and guaranteeing RMBS and may replace its existing portfolio of retained mortgages, RMBS, and tranches of CMOs.
3. The FHFA suspended dividends on existing common and preferred shares in both GSEs.
4. The FHFA stopped all lobbying and political activities in both GSEs. The FHFA will review all charitable contributions in both GSEs.

At same time, Secretary Paulson announced that the Treasury was making substantial equity investments in both GSEs.

1. The Treasury purchased (1) $1 billion of senior preferred stock in each GSE, and (2) warrants to buy up to 79.9 percent of the common shares in each GSE at a nominal price.
2. The Treasury committed to invest up to $100 billion in each GSE. If the FHFA determines that the liabilities in either GSE exceed its assets at the end of a quarter, the Treasury will contribute cash equal to the difference. In return, the Treasury's senior preferred stock will increase by the same amount.
3. The senior preferred stock will accrue dividends of 10 percent. Dividends will increase to 12 percent in any quarter in which dividends are not paid

in cash and will remain at this rate until all accrued dividends have been paid in cash.

4. Beginning on March 31, 2010, each GSE will pay a quarterly commitment fee to Treasury that will be determined jointly by the FHFA and the Treasury.
5. Each GSE requires the prior consent of the Treasury to:

a. Issue stock, redeem stock, or pay dividends (except on the Treasury's senior preferred stock);
b. Sell, transfer, or dispose of assets outside of the normal course of business;
c. Acquire, be acquired, or merge with other companies;
d. Incur total debt in excess of 110 percent of its total debt on June 30, 2008; and
e. Terminate the conservatorship.

6. As of December 31, 2009, each GSE must limit its portfolio of retained mortgages, RMBS, and tranches of CMOs to $850 billion. Thereafter, each GSE must reduce its portfolio by 10 percent a year until its portfolio is less than $250 billion.

Secretary Paulson announced the creation of a Government-Sponsored Enterprise Credit Facility (GSECF) that would remain in effect until December 31, 2009.

1. Fannie Mae, Freddie Mac, and the Federal Home Loan Board Banks (FHLB) may borrow from the Treasury through the GSECF based on collateral consisting of GSE-issued RMBS or FHLB advances.
2. All loans will be short-term and have maturities before January 1, 2010.
3. The interest rate will be the London interbank offer rate (LIBOR) plus 50 basis points.
4. The Federal Reserve Bank of New York will value and manage the collateral.

Secretary Paulson also announced the Treasury would purchase up to $5 billion of GSE-issued RMBS on the open market through December 31, 2008. The Treasury intends to hold these RMBS until maturity.

LEHMAN BROTHERS

Lehman Brothers was the fourth largest independent investment bank in the United States. During the weekend of September 13-14, 2008, Federal Reserve and Treasury officials determined that Lehman Brothers was probably insolvent. Both Bank of America and Barclays broke off negotiations to acquire Lehman Brothers when Federal Reserve and Treasury officials made it clear that the federal government would not assist any buyers of Lehman Brothers.

On Monday September 15, 2008, Lehman Brothers filed for Chapter 11 (reorganization) bankruptcy. In the bankruptcy filing, the firm listed debts of $613 billion and assets of $639 billion. Because of the bankruptcy, mutual funds (including funds sponsored by Franklin Advisers, Pimco, and Vanguard) are expected to lose at least $86 billion of their $143 billion investment in Lehman Brothers debt securities.

On Tuesday September 16, 2008, Barclays agreed to buy Lehman Brothers' U.S. investment banking unit for $1.75 billion, saving about 9,000 jobs. Other units are currently for sale.

On Monday September 22, 2008, Noruma Holdings, Japan's largest investment bank, agreed to buy the Asian operations of Lehman Brothers for $225 million.

MERRILL LYNCH

Once the negotiations to acquire Lehman Brothers broke down, Bank of America began negotiations to acquire Merrill Lynch. On Monday September 15, 2008, Bank of America announced that it planned to acquire Merrill Lynch by exchanging 0.8595 shares of its common stock for each Merrill Lynch common share, valuing Merrill Lynch at $29 a share. The total value of this acquisition is $44 billion. On Friday September 12, 2008, Merrill Lynch closed at $17.05 a share.

AMERICAN INTERNATIONAL GROUP (AIG)

AIG is the world's largest insurer with 74 million customers in 130 countries and $1.04 trillion of assets. AIG encountered severe liquidity problems primarily because of uncertainty about the ultimate size of the losses in its portfolio of credit default swaps (CDS) for subprime RMBS and CMOs and the resulting erosion of AIG's capital. AIG has outstanding CDS of $441 billion. AIG's losses have been heavily concentrated in the capital markets segment of its financial services division that underwrote CDS. AIG has also suffered smaller losses in mortgage insurance. In addition to recognized losses, Morgan Stanley estimated that AIG has unrealized losses of $24 billion. Other AIG units (i.e., life insurance and retirement services, general insurance, and asset management) and other segments in financial services (i.e., consumer finance and aircraft leasing) are profitable.

Over the weekend of September 13-14, 2008, credit rating agencies threatened to downgrade AIG unless it could raise $40 billion through asset sales. On Monday morning September 15, 2008, New York Governor David Patterson permitted AIG to upstream $20 billion from its regulated insurance subsidiaries to the parent firm until asset sales could be completed. On Monday afternoon, the Federal Reserve (1) refused to provide a $40 billion bridge loan to AIG, and instead (2) tasked JPMorganChase and Goldman Sachs to secure $75 billion in private bridge financing for AIG. On Monday night, however, A. M. Best, Fitch, Moody's, and Standard & Poor's downgraded AIG.[3] These downgrades triggered $14.5 billion of additional collateral requirements, and contract terminations requiring payments of $5.4 billion.

On Tuesday September 16, 2008, investors paid $5.2 million up front plus $500,000 annually to protect $10 million of AIG debt against default for five years, up from $3.3 million up front on Monday. Thus, the market thought AIG's bankruptcy was inevitable without federal government assistance.

That day, it became clear that AIG could not secure bridge financing from private sources. Federal Reserve and Treasury officials concluded that AIG's bankruptcy "could add to already significant levels of financial market fragility and lead to substantially higher borrowing costs, reduced household wealth, and materially weaker economic performance." RBC Capital Markets analyst Hank Calenti estimated that AIG's bankruptcy would cause $180 billion of additional losses in financial firms.

Since financial firms are currently having difficulty raising capital, Federal Reserve and Treasury officials feared that additional losses at this time could force many banks to contract their lending, aggravating the economic downturn. Moreover, many money market mutual funds own short-term AIG debt securities. Federal Reserve and Treasury officials feared that AIG's bankruptcy would cause a number of money market mutual funds to "break the buck" (i.e., its net asset value fell below $ 1-a-share level), possibly triggering widespread panic.

Because of these fears, the Federal Reserve decided to provide an $85 billion bridge loan to AIG for 24 months at a floating interest rate of 3- month LIBOR plus 850 basis points (equal to 11.38 percent on Tuesday September 16, 2008). AIG pledged all of its assets, including the stock in its subsidiaries, as collateral. AIG will repay the loan through asset sales. The risk to the Federal Reserve from this loan is minimal since analysts believe the AIG's break-up value is substantially greater than the loan amount. For example, Bijan Moazami, an analyst at Friedman, Billings, Ramsey, estimated that AIG has a break-up value of $150 billion.

In exchange, the Federal Reserve received warrants to purchase up to 79.9 percent of AIG's common shares at a nominal price. The Federal Reserve must approve any dividends paid on AIG's common or preferred shares while the loan is outstanding. At the insistence of Secretary Paulson, former Allstate CEO Edward Liddy replaced Robert Willumstad as AIG's CEO.

Federal Reserve

In the wake of the bankruptcy of Lehman Brothers, the Federal Reserve took a number of steps to relieve the severe liquidity stress in credit markets:

1. On Sunday September 14, 2008, the Federal Reserve:

   a. Expanded the eligible collateral for the Primary Dealer Credit Facility[4] to include non-investment debt securities and equity securities;
   b. Expanded the eligible collateral for the Term Securities Lending Facility[5] to include all investment-grade debt securities;[6]
   c. Increased the total funds available under the Term Securities Lending Facility from $175 billion to $200 billion; and
   d. Organized a consortium of 10 banks to lend up to $7 billion each for a total of $70 billion to financial firms that come under liquidity stress because of the bankruptcy of Lehman Brothers.

2. On Monday September 15, 2008, the Federal Reserve injected $20 billion into financial markets through open market operations.
3. On Tuesday September 16, 2008, the Federal Reserve left its target federal funds rate unchanged at 2.00 percent. However, the Federal Reserve injected $50 billion of liquidity into financial markets through open market operations. Simultaneously, the Bank of Japan, the Bank of England, and the European Central Bank injected $23.8 billion, $36 billion, and $100.2 billion, respectively.

4. On Wednesday September 17, 2008, the Treasury announced a Supplementary Financing Program to sell additional Treasury bills beyond the federal government's funding needs to provide cash to the Federal Reserve. The initial amount was $40 billion.
5. For the week ending on Wednesday September 17, 2008, the Federal Reserve increased:

a. Loans to commercial banks and other depository institutions from $23.6 billion to $33.5 billion;
b. Loans to Primary Dealers (i.e., independent investment banks) from zero to $59.8 billion; and
c. Overnight and term securities lent to Primary Dealers from $117.3 billion to $127.3 billion.

6. At 3 a.m. EDST on Thursday September 18, 2008, the Federal Reserve expanded its currency swap lines with the European Central Bank by $55 billion to $110 billion and with the Swiss National Bank by $15 billion to $27 billion. The Federal Reserve established swap lines with the Bank of Japan ($60 billion), the Bank of England ($40 billion), and the Bank of Canada ($10 billion). This allowed the European Central Bank to auction $40 billion in short-term U.S. dollar credit to European banks. Moreover, the Federal Reserve injected an additional $55 billion of liquidity into financial markets through open market operations.

Despite these aggressive measures to relieve stress in credit markets, financial firms hoarded what liquidity they had and scrambled for more. This caused the federal funds rate to peak at 6 percent, far above its target rate of 2 percent. Moreover, overnight rates for loans between banks spiked (see Figure 1).

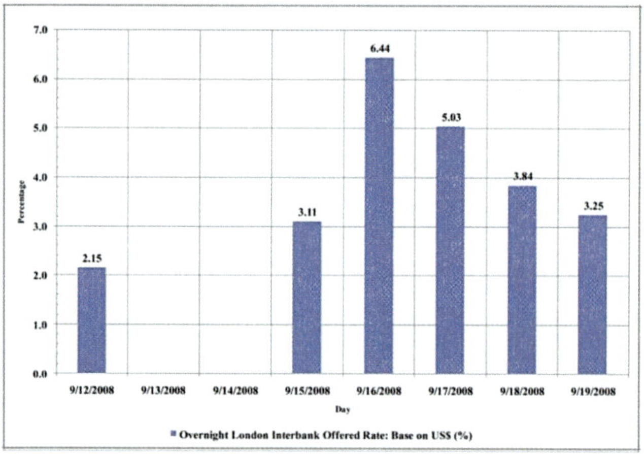

Figure 1. Overnight LIBOR — September 12-19, 2008

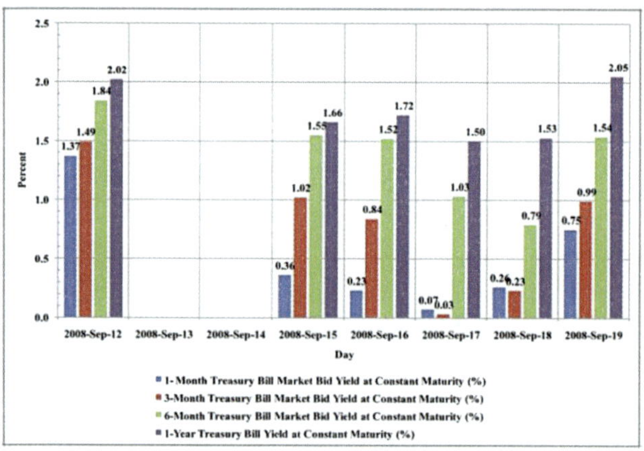

Figure 2. hort-Term Treasury Bill Yields — September 12-19, 2008

Despite these aggressive measures to relieve stress in credit markets, financial firms hoarded what liquidity they had and scrambled for more. This caused the federal funds rate to peak at 6 percent, far above its target rate of 2 percent. Moreover, overnight rates for loans between banks spiked (see Figure 1).

There was a general flight to quality that produced extraordinary demand for Treasury debt securities. Consequently, short-term Treasury yields fell to levels not seen in more than fifty years (see Figure 2).

FINANCIAL PRECIPICE

The United States was on the edge of a financial precipice. Private credit markets began to seize up. The issuance of investment-grade corporate bonds and commercial paper virtually ceased.

Overnight borrowing costs for major corporations soared. *The Wall Street Journal* reported Ford Motor Credit paid 7.5 percent for its overnight borrowing compared with the 2.5 percent that it would normally pay with a 2 percent target for the federal funds rate. General Electric paid 3.5 percent.

Share prices dropped worldwide. On Monday September 15, 2008, the Dow Jones Industrial Average fell by 505 points, or 4.4 percent, to close at 10,917 points. On Tuesday, the Dow Jones Industrial Average rose by 142 points, or 1.3 percent, to close at 11,059 points. On Wednesday, the Dow Jones Industrial Average fell by 449 points, or 4.1 percent, to close at 10,610 points.

Short sellers launched bear raids that drove down the shares of Goldman Sachs and Morgan Stanley. During intraday trading on Thursday September 18, 2008, Goldman Sachs fell to 88.69, down 42.5 percent from its close on Friday September 12, 2008, while Morgan Stanley dropped to 11.92, down 63.3 percent from its Friday close.

In response to its perilous condition, Morgan Stanley simultaneously (1) entered into merger negotiations with Wachovia, and (2) approached the Chinese government for a large equity infusion from the PRC's sovereign wealth fund or its state- owned financial institutions. This could increase the PRC's equity interest in Morgan Stanley from less than 9.9 percent up to 49.9 percent.

Shares continued to plunge on Thursday September 18, 2008. The Dow Jones Industrial Average reached an intraday low of 10,459 points. Then, during the last hour of trade, Charlie Gasparino broke the story on CNBC that:

1. Chairman Bernanke and Secretary Paulson were favorably disposed to a "good bank, bad bank," Resolution Trust Corporation (RTC)- type plan to buy and dispose of bad mortgage- related financial assets; and
2. They would present this plan to Congressional leaders later in the day.

The Dow Jones Industrial Average skyrocketed from its intraday low and closed up 410 points, or 3.9 percent, to 11,020.

Breaking the Buck Causes Runs on Money Market Mutual Funds

On Monday September 15, 2008, the $62 billion Reserve Primary Fund, a money market mutual fund, "broke the buck" because of its investment in Lehman Brothers' short-term debt securities. The Reserve Primary Fund suspended redemptions for one week.

On June 30, 2008, money market mutual funds had total assets of $3.3 trillion of assets. Among these assets, money market mutual funds held $701 billion of commercial paper, or about 40 percent of all commercial paper outstanding. "Breaking the buck" at the Reserve Primary Fund caused investors to question unnecessarily the soundness of other money market mutual funds.

Irrational runs on money market mutual funds began. For the week ending on Wednesday September 17, 2008, investors redeemed $145 billion from their money market mutual funds. On Thursday September 18, 2008, institutional money managers sought to redeem another $500 billion, but Secretary Paulson intervened directly with these managers to dissuade them from demanding redemptions. Nevertheless, investors still redeemed another $105 billion. If the federal government were not to act decisively to check this incipient panic, the results for the entire U.S. economy would be disastrous.

1. To satisfy redemptions, money market mutual funds slashed their holdings of commercial paper. Commercial paper outstanding fell by $52 billion during the week ending on Wednesday September 17, 2008 as money market funds refused to rollover commercial paper. If this trend continued, major nonfinancial firms would

a. Lose their primary source for short-term borrowing, and
b. Call upon their back-up lines of credit with commercial banks.

2. Given the extreme funding problems commercial banks were encountering during the week, commercial banks would either:

a. Slash credit to small- and medium-size nonfinancial firms and households to meet the line of credit commitments to large nonfinancial firms, or
b. Not be able to fulfill the line of credit commitments to large non-financial firms at all.

3. The result would be a disabling credit contraction that would trigger a severe and lengthy recession with large declines in production and employment, further erosion in household wealth, and a significant

increase in the federal budget deficit as countercyclical outlays soared and tax receipts dwindled.

BIRTH OF A COMPREHENSIVE PLAN

This run forced Chairman Bernanke and Secretary Paulson to reassess the federal government's previous *ad hoc* approach to the global financial crisis. Together Bernanke and Paulson concluded a comprehensive plan was necessary to (1) restore confidence and (2) kick start credit markets into functioning again.

To stop the runs on money market mutual funds and to revive the market for commercial paper, Chairman Bernanke and Secretary Paulson acted swiftly on Friday September 19, 2008.

1. Secretary Paulson announced a temporary program through which the Treasury will use the $50 billion in the Exchange Stabilization Fund to protect investors in money market mutual funds from any losses should their fund "break the buck" during the next year. Money market mutual funds will pay an insurance premium to the Treasury for this guarantee.
2. The Federal Reserve established two loan facilities to help money market mutual funds meet any demand for redemptions.

a. The Federal Reserve will extend non-recourse loans of up to $230 billion to banks and other depository institutions to buy investment-grade asset-backed commercial paper from money market mutual funds.
b. The Federal Reserve will extend non-recourse loans to primary dealers of up to $69 billion to buy short-term debt securities of Fannie Mae, Freddie Mac, or FHLBs from money market mutual funds.

During Thursday evening September 18, 2008, Chairman Bernanke and Secretary Paulson discussed their proposal for a comprehensive plan to solve the global financial crisis with Congressional leaders. As initially proposed, the plan would:

1. Authorize the Treasury to purchase up to $700 billion (equal to 4.9 percent of GDP) of impaired mortgage-related financial assets including residential mortgage loans, commercial mortgage loans, RMBS, commercial mortgage-backed securities (CMBS), or CMOs from U.S.-headquartered financial institutions; and

2. Authorize the Treasury to manage and dispose of these assets in manner promote stability in financial markets and protects the interests of taxpayers.

In addition, the Treasury announced that it was increasing the size of its previously announced purchase of GSE-issued RMBS from $5 billion to $10 billion.

At the same time, securities regulators around the world temporarily tightened their restrictions on short sales. On Thursday September 18, 2008, the Financial Services Authority placed a temporary ban on short sales of financial services stocks in United Kingdom. On the same day, the Securities and Exchange Commission (SEC) strengthened its rule about covered short sales. On Friday September 19, 2008, the SEC also placed a temporary ban on short sales of the stocks of 799 financial services firms through October 2, 2008.

Stress in credit market conditions finally began to easy on Friday. The overnight LIBOR fell from 3.84 percent on Thursday September 18, 2008 to 3.25 percent on Friday September 19, 2008.

Stock markets around the world rallied on this news. On Friday September 19, 2008, the Dow Jones Industrial Average rose by 369 points, or 3.3 percent, closed at 11,388 points. Despite a wild ride, the Dow Jones Industrial Average was down only 0.3 percent on the week. However, the overnight LIBOR remains 110 basis points higher than a week ago.

As of the writing of this research report, there are a number of question about the plan that Chairman Bernanke and Secretary Paulson have yet to answer:

1. How will the Treasury buy these impaired financial assets? Reports suggest that the Treasury is planning to use reverse auctions.
2. What price will the Treasury pay for these impaired financial assets? If the Treasury pays the deeply discounted price indicated by fair value accounting, the Treasury may earn a profit over time on the disposition of these impaired financial assets. If the Treasury pays a substantially higher price, the Treasury will effectively subsidize the financial institutions that are selling these impaired financial assets, and the Treasury will be more likely to incur losses on the disposition of these impaired financial assets.
3. How will the Treasury dispose of impaired financial assets? Will the Treasury immediately repackage and resell some of these assets to long-term investors? Or will the Treasury hold these assets until maturity?
4. Will the Treasury facilitate the restructuring of impaired residential mortgage loans by reducing the principal balance to a reasonable percent

of the current value of the collateral and lowering the interest rate to help financially stressed borrowers stay in their homes?

WEEKEND AND MONDAY DEVELOPMENTS

Several important developments occurred over the weekend of September 20-21, 2008 and on Monday September 22, 2008.

1. Secretary Paulson agreed to several changes to the initial plan:

   a. The Treasury would be authorized to expand to purchase all impaired financial assets, not just mortgage-related financial assets;
   b. The Treasury would be authorized to purchase impaired financial assets from foreign-based financial institutions with substantial operations within the United States; and
   c. An oversight board would monitor the implementation of the plan.

2. As for the federal guarantee of money market mutual funds,

   a. Secretary Paulson limited the federal guarantee of money market mutual funds to accounts in existence as of September 19, 2008. New accounts opened thereafter would not be covered by the federal guarantee.
   b. Secretary Paulson extended the federal guarantee to tax-exempt money market mutual funds that invest exclusively in short-term municipal debt securities.

3. Certain policymakers are currently pressing the Treasury to agree to:

   a. Taking an equity stake in any financial institution from which the Treasury purchases impaired financial assets;
   b. Limiting compensation in any financial institution from which the Treasury purchases impaired financial assets;
   c. Amending bankruptcy law to allow judge to reduce mortgage loan balances; and
   d. Supporting additional programs to help delinquent homeowners to remain in their residences.

4. On Monday September 21, 2008, *The Wall Street Journal* reported an agreement between Congressional leaders and Treasury that the Treasury could acquire, but would not be required to acquire, warrants in financial

firms from which the Treasury buys impaired financial assets. Other differences remain unresolved.

5. On Sunday September 21, 2008, both Goldman Sachs and Morgan Stanley received emergency approval from the Federal Reserve to become Bank Holding Companies (BHCs). As of Friday September 26, 2008, there will be no independent major investment banks in the United States.

a. As BHCs, both firms may open or acquire commercial banks and are eligible to borrow from the Federal Reserve. Moreover, the Federal Reserve becomes their primary federal regulator instead of the SEC.
   (i) Goldman Sachs, which had $20 billion of deposits in two subsidiaries, will establish GS Bank USA.
   (ii) Morgan Stanley, which had $36 billion of deposits in its Utah-based industrial bank, will convert it into a national bank.
b. Analysts expect both Goldman Sachs and Morgan Stanley to continue reducing leverage and raising capital.
   (i) Morgan Stanley ended merger negotiations with Wachovia. On Monday September 22, 2008, Mitsubishi UFJ Financial Group Inc. agreed to invest up to $8.4 billion in Morgan Stanley for an equity stake of between 10 percent and 20 percent.

6. On Monday September 28, 2008, the Federal Reserve narrowed its presumption of control rule to allow private equity firms to make larger equity investments in banks without becoming subject to regulation as a bank holding company. This expands the pool of capital available to banks and their holding companies.
7. On Monday September 28, 2008, the SEC expanded its temporary ban on short sales by adding 71 corporations, including General Electric, General Motors, and other corporations with large financial subsidiaries. Many other developed countries have adopted similar temporary bans on short sales. The SEC also limited the scope of its ban by allowing traders in *bona fide* market making and hedging activities to short.

The Friday's euphoria dissipated as economists and financial analysts cautioned that Paulson's plan (1) will be costly, (2) cannot immediately stop the decline in U.S. housing prices, and (3) will take months, if not years, to work. On Monday September 22, 2008, the Dow Jones Industrial Average fell by 373 points, or 3.3 percent, to close at 11,016 points. The U.S. dollar also fell in foreign exchange markets over mounting fears about the deterioration in the federal government's fiscal position.

HEDGE FUNDS

Independent investment banks have been a major source of short-term credit to hedge funds through secured lines of credit and repurchase agreements. As of December 31, 2007, prime brokers provided hedge funds $1.4 trillion to support $2.7 trillion in assets. Formerly independent investment banks will continue to sell financial assets and liabilities to reduce their leverage ratios as they adjust to their new status as or within bank holding companies. Thus, the short- term credit that had been readily available to hedge funds may contract significantly. This contraction may force some hedge funds into bankruptcy.

CONCLUSION

Much of the alternative financial system imploded during September 2008. Fannie Mae and Freddie Mac have been placed into conservatorships. As of September 26, 2008, there will not be any independent major investment banks. There was very little that any policymaker could have done to stop this collapse once the financial dominos began to fall. The Federal Reserve and the Treasury have intervened deftly in credit markets to limit the damage to the broader U.S. economy.

End Notes

[1] Robert P. O'Quinn, *The U.S. Housing Bubble and the Global Financial Crisis: Housing and Housing-Related Finance*, JEC Study, 110th Cong., 2nd sess., May 2008. Found at http://www.house.gov/jec/news/Housing%20Bubble%20 study.pdf; and Robert P. O'Quinn, *The U.S. Housing Bubble and the Global Financial Crisis: Vulnerabilities of the Alternative Financial System*, JEC Study, 1 10th Cong., 2nd sess., May 2008. Found at http://www.house.gov/jec/studies/2008/The_US_Housin g Bubble June 2008 Study.pdf.

[2] Walter Bagehot, *Lombard Street: A Description of the Money Market* (Homewood, IL: R. D. Irwin, 1963 [1873]).

[3] Fitch cut AIG's rating two notches to A from AA- minus. Moody's Investors Service reduced AIG's rating two notches to A2 from Aa3. Standard & Poor's slashed AIG's long-term credit rating three notches to A-minus from AA-minus.

[4] The Primary Dealer Credit Facility provides short-term loans to investment banks.

[5] The Term Securities Lending Facility allows investment banks to borrow Treasuries debt securities in exchange for other eligible debt securities.

[6] Previously, only Treasury debt securities, agency debt securities, and AAA-rated mortgage-backed and asset- backed securities were eligible.

In: Economic Crises as a Result of Distrust
Editors: Emilio Gullini ISBN: 978-1-60741-355-4

Chapter 6

GOVERNMENT POLICY BLUNDERS AND GLOBAL FINANCIAL CRISIS

Jim Saxton

Macroeconomic and microeconomic policy blunders by both the U.S. government and foreign governments inflated an unsustainable housing bubble in the United States and other developed economies. When this bubble inevitably popped, a global financial crisis ensued. Although misaligned private incentives, methodological errors in rating structured credit products, and the recklessness of some private financial institutions and investors did play a contributory role in the recent financial turmoil, individuals and firms could not have created and sustained such a large housing bubble over so long a time without major macroeconomic and microeconomic policy mistakes. These policy mistakes were:

1. The exchange rate policy of the People's Republic of China (PRC) and the shadow exchange rate policies of governments in other Asian economies caused large and persistent international trade imbalances, suppressed price increases on tradable goods and services, and channeled monetary inflation in the United States and other developed countries with floating exchange rates disproportionately into housing prices;
2. The Federal Reserve pursued, at least in retrospect, an overly accommodative monetary policy after 2000 that kept U.S. interest rates too low for too long. Moreover, central banks in the PRC and other Asian economies invested most of their surging foreign exchange reserves in

U.S. Treasury, Fannie Mae, and Freddie Mac debt securities, flatting the long-end of the yield curve in the United States. These policies combined to produce extremely low long-term interest rates that stimulated housing demand.

3. Financial regulators in the United States and other developed economies failed to exercise adequate prudential supervision over highly leveraged non-depository financial institutions in the alternative financial system;
4. Regulations mandating the use of value-at-risk models to determine the capital adequacy of financial institutions (1) caused both these institutions and their regulators to underestimate risk exposure, and (2) encouraged these institutions to increase their leverage;
5. Regulations mandating the use of "fair value" accounting (also known as "mark-to-market" accounting) for illiquid financial assets exacerbated liquidity problems at financial institutions after the housing bubble burst.
6. The strengthening of affordable housing regulations governing Fannie Mae and Freddie Mac in October 2000 had the unintended consequence of creating a large regulatory- induced demand for subprime residential mortgage loans that mortgage banks proceeded to satisfy.[1]

MACROECONOMIC POLICY FACTORS

During the last decade, the governments of the world's major economies have pursued two different exchange rate policies: freely floating exchange rates and pegged exchange rates. In the "floating zone," the United States along with Australia, Canada, the European Union member-states using the euro, and the United Kingdom allowed market forces to determine the foreign exchange value of their currencies. In the "pegging zone," the People's Republic of China (PRC), Indonesia, India, Japan, South Korea, Malaysia, Taiwan, and Thailand intervened heavily in the foreign exchange market by buying dollars and selling their currencies to maintain politically determined, below market exchange rates pegged to the U.S. dollar to give their manufactured exports a price advantage in American and European markets.

Pegged exchange rates produced persistent distortions in relative prices around the world. Over time, these price distortions exacerbated imbalances in the global economy, especially large, persistent current account surpluses in the PRC and large, persistent current account deficits in United States.

Consequently, the governments of these Asian economies added $2.7 trillion to their foreign exchange reserves between December 31, 2000 and December 31,

2007. About 70 percent of this increase in foreign exchange reserves was invested in the United States, mostly in U.S. Treasury debt securities and U.S. Agency debt securities (e.g., Fannie Mae and Freddie Mac).

The exchange rate-induced price distortions influenced macroeconomic policy decision-making around the world. In the United States and other economies in the floating zone, central banks pursued, at least in retrospect, overly accommodative monetary policies that expanded the availability of credit at low interest rates. In turn, these policies inflated unsustainable housing price bubbles. In the PRC and some other economies in the pegging zone, macroeconomic policy errors caused price inflation in goods and services to surge.

After these housing bubbles popped, massive overinvestment (i.e., the accumulation of assets in excess of the demand for these assets) and malinvestment (i.e., the accumulation of the wrong types of assets) was revealed in the housing sectors of the United States and most of the other major economies in the floating zone. This triggered a global financial crisis that began on August 9, 2007.

Specifically:

1. Low-cost imports, especially labor-intensive manufactured goods from the pegging zone, intensified competition for tradable goods in the United States and other economies in the floating zone. Because of this competition, various indices used to measure changes in the prices of goods and services registered very low inflation rates in the United States and other economies in the floating zone.
2. Low reported inflation rates persuaded officials at the Federal Reserve and other central banks to pursue relatively accommodative monetary policies throughout most of the last decade.
3. Because asset prices are generally excluded from inflation indices, higher housing prices did not increase reported inflation rates and did not trigger more restrictive monetary policies in the United States or other economies in the floating zone.
4. At least in retrospect, the Federal Reserve and other central banks in the floating zone pursued overly accommodate monetary policies during most of the last decade. This fed a rapid expansion of credit relative to GDP. In the United States, total credit outstanding (including total debt securities outstanding in U.S. credit markets and total loans and leases outstanding at U.S. depository institutions) grew from $17.1 trillion

(equal to 205.8 percent of GDP) on December 31, 1997 to $38.3 trillion (equal to 276.8 percent of GDP) on December 31, 2007.

5. Central banks in the pegging zone invested a large portion of their accumulation of foreign exchange reserves in medium- and long-term U.S. Treasury debt securities and U.S. Agency debt securities. These investment decisions flattened the yield curve in the United States, pushing medium- and long-term U.S. interest rates below what they would have otherwise been. Of course, the housing sector is especially sensitive to changes in long-term interest rates.

MICROECONOMIC POLICY FACTORS

During the last three decades, an alternative financial system has developed to the traditional bank-centric financial system. This alternative system is based on (1) the securitization of loans, leases, and receivables into structured credit products (e.g., residential mortgage-backed securities), and (2) the purchase of these structured credit products by highly leveraged non-depository financial institutions (e.g., investment banks, financial government-sponsored enterprises including Fannie Mae and Freddie Mac, hedge funds, and off-balance sheet entities).

Highly leveraged non-depository financial institutions now perform the same economically vital, but inherently risky functions of (1) intermediation[2] and (2) liquidity and maturity transformation[3] that banks, savings institutions, and credit unions have historically performed. In the United States at the end of 2007, highly leveraged non-depository financial institutions held $12.7 trillion of financial assets compared with $13.5 trillion of financial assets in depository institutions.

However, this alternative system, which developed largely outside of the regulatory and supervisory structure that has been necessary to contain financial contagion, proved vulnerable to a modern version of 19th century bank runs. Instead of depositors "running" to banks to withdraw their deposits, unleveraged financial institutions such as money market mutual funds that lose confidence in highly leveraged non-depository financial institutions (e.g., Bear Stearns) refuse to rollover their overnight repurchase agreements while banks curtail their secured lines of credit, forcing such troubled institutions to either declare bankruptcy or seek government assistance in a matter of hours.

UNINTENDED CONSEQUENCES FROM FINANCIAL REGULATIONS

Federal regulatory policies that addressed legitimate problems (i.e., inconsistent capital regulations for multinational banks, and inadequate accounting standards that allowed Enron to conceal its true financial condition before its collapse in 2001) had the unintended consequences of encouraging excessive leverage and risk-taking especially among these highly leveraged non-depository financial institutions. In particular, two policies encouraged financial institutions to behave pro-cyclically:

1. Promoting the use of value-at-risk models to determine the risk exposure in financial institutions without sufficient consideration of the inherent limitations in these models, especially the lack of sufficient historical data to draw statistically valid conclusions about (a) the credit performance of new products, and (b) institutional liquidity under rare episodes of financial stress; and
2. Requiring financial institutions to use fair value (also known as mark-to-market) accounting for illiquid financial assets that such institutions intend to hold.

Reliance on value-at-risk models caused both financial institutions and their regulators to underestimate the risk exposure at these institutions. This underestimation encouraged aggressive lending and underwriting practices at financial institutions during upswings.

Small changes in the price factors that econometric models use to estimate the fair value of illiquid financial assets can cause large drops in the recorded value of these assets during downturns, forcing financial institutions to take large write-downs. These write-downs can trigger "fire sales," in which financial institutions rush to sell similar financial assets at any price, possibly reducing the value of these assets well below what they actually fetch during orderly sales. Widespread illiquidity may force financial institutions to contract the availability of credit and increase its cost.

Unintended Consequences from Housing Policies Promoting Home Ownership

The shift from FHA-insured mortgage loans to subprime mortgage loans among low income households in the United States and the widespread issuance of subprime mortgage-backed securities by investment banks during the first half of this decade is, in large part, the unintended consequence of well-meaning, but poorly conceived federal policies to increase the home ownership rate among low income households. On October 31, 2000, the U.S. Secretary of Housing and Urban Development issued affordable housing regulations for Fannie Mae and Freddie Mac during the years 2001 to 2004. These regulations significantly increased the goals at Fannie Mae and Freddie Mac for purchasing residential mortgage loans to low income households. To meet these goals, Fannie Mae and Freddie Mac stepped-up their purchases of privately issued AAA-rated tranches of subprime mortgage-backed securities beginning in 2001. Responding to this regulatory-induced demand, mortgage banks greatly increased their extension of subprime mortgage loans, while investment banks placed these loans into subprime mortgage-backed securities.

Misaligned Private Incentives

Misaligned private incentives encouraged excessive risk-taking in financial institutions:

1. Unlike the originators of other loans, leases, or receivables, the originators of residential mortgage loans were not required to retain an equity interest, known as "skin in the game," in (a) the loans which were sold or (b) the mortgage-backed securities into which these loans were placed. Thus, originators such as mortgage banks had no incentive to apply sound credit standards when underwriting residential mortgage loans.
2. The "issuer pays" business model of credit rating agencies made them financially dependent upon a few investment banks whose structured credit products the agencies were assessing. These agencies pressed their analysts to give favorable ratings to maintain or increase market share with these banks.

3. Banks had "up-front" incentive compensation packages for investment bankers that did not adjust their compensation for the long-term profitability of their deals for the banks or their customers.

METHODOLOGICAL ERRORS

Credit rating agencies employed flawed methodologies to evaluate structured credit products. These methodologies did not fully account for the likely correlation of delinquency and default rates for similar loans, leases, and receivables that constitute the collateral in structured credit products. This error caused credit rating agencies to give higher ratings to many structured credit products than they deserved.

CONCLUSION

Macroeconomic policy errors both here and abroad combined with regulatory policy deficiencies and misaligned private incentives to inflate unsustainable bubbles in housing prices in the United States and most of the other major economies in the floating zone. After these bubbles popped, the alternative financial system proved vulnerable to a modern version of 19th century bank runs. This sparked a global financial crisis that is ongoing.

End Notes

[1] For more detailed analyses, see: Robert P. O'Quinn, *Chinese FX Interventions Caused International Imbalances, Contributed to the U.S. Housing Bubble*, Prepared for the Joint Economic Committee (110th Cong., 2nd sess., March 2008); Robert P. O'Quinn, *The U.S. Housing Bubble and the Global Financial Crisis: Housing and Housing-Related Finance*, Prepared for the Joint Economic (110th Cong., 2nd sess., May 2008); and Robert P. O'Quinn, *The U.S. Housing Bubble and the Global Financial Crisis: Vulnerabilities of the Alternative Financial System,* Prepared for the Joint Economic Committee (110th Cong., 2nd sess., June 2008).

[2] Intermediation refers the economic function of channeling funds from savers to borrowers.

[3] Liquidity and maturity transformation refers to the economic function of turning illiquid financial assets such as term loans to households and firms into liquid financial assets such as deposits payable on demand or marketable securities.

In: Economic Crises as a Result of Distrust
Editors: Emilio Gullini
ISBN: 978-1-60741-355-4

Chapter 7

HOOVER'S LETHAL ECONOMIC POLICY MIX

Jim Saxton

The popping of the housing bubble, the subsequent increases in residential mortgage loan delinquency and foreclosure rates, and the recent failures of commercial and investment banks have prompted some Americans to suggest that current economic policies are similar to Herbert Hoover's.

To assess the validity of this assertion, one must first understand what Hoover's economic policies actually were. There is a widespread misconception that under Hoover the federal government remained idle as the economy contracted. In reality, Hoover aggressively pursued bad economic policies that transformed what could have been at worst a short recession into the worst depression in U.S. history.

Although Hoover did not understand banking, finance, and monetary policy, his success as an engineer, entrepreneur, and government official prior to his inauguration convinced him that he did not require economic advice. Hoover thought that he already knew everything that there was to know about economics. Hoover's arrogance proved disastrous. Hoover repeatedly ignored sound advice from prominent economists to pursue relentlessly bad economic policies based on his wrong-headed notions, his quirky morality, and his anti-bank, anti-Wall Street prejudices.

Monetary Causes of the 1920s Stock Market Bubble and its Popping

Ignoring the shift of wealth that had occurred during World War I, Chancellor of the Exchequer Winston Churchill mistakenly returned the British pound to the gold standard at its pre-war mint price in 1925. At their pre-war mint prices, the U.S. dollar was undervalued, and the British pound was overvalued, producing persistent U.S. current account surpluses and persistent British current account deficits.

The first Governor of the Federal Reserve Bank of New York Benjamin Strong, who had assumed *de facto* control of U.S. monetary policy until his death in October 1928, pressed the Federal Reserve to lower U.S. interest rates, even though the Federal temper a booming U.S. economy. Strong thought that lower U.S. interest rates would help the Bank of England maintain the gold standard at its pre-war mint price by encouraging financial flows from the United States to the United Kingdom that would partially offset Britain's current account deficit and would therefore reduce Britain's gold outflows. Economists now blame Strong's inappropriate monetary policy for the stock market bubble in 1928 and the first eight months of 1929 and the reversal of this policy after his death for the popping of the stock bubble in October 1929.

From a high of 381.17 on September 3, 1929, the Dow Jones Industrial Average dropped to 298.17 on October 24, 1929 and plunged to 230.17 on October 29, 1929. Seeking villains to demonize, Hoover instinctively blamed the crash in share prices on speculators and their short sales. Hoover urged Congress to launch investigations into the speculators and then proceeded to make an unprecedented series of economic policy blunders.

Acquiescence in Monetary Contraction and Three Rounds of Bank Failures

Noble laureate Milton Friedman assigned the blame for the unprecedented economic collapse between August 1929 and March 1933 to the Federal Reserve's misguided policy of monetary contraction.[1] Hoover could have forced the Federal Reserve to change its policy. Prior to 1935, two of the seven members of the Federal Reserve Board, the Secretary of the Treasury and the Comptroller of the Currency, served at the pleasure of the president, while the remaining five members were presidential appointees with staggered ten-year terms.[2]

Unfortunately, Hoover and a majority of his appointees still subscribed to the spurious "real bills" doctrine of monetary policy[3] that British economist Walter Bagehot had discredited nearly a half-century earlier in *Lombard Street*.[4] Hoover dismissed numerous warnings from prominent economists such as Irving Fisher that the Federal Reserve should stop contracting the money supply. Moreover, Hoover's appointees repeatedly rejected the pleas of George Harrison, the Governor of the Federal Reserve Bank of New York, to reverse the monetary contraction.

The collapse of outward U.S. foreign investment in 1929 caused a large inflow of gold into the United States during the next two years.[5] Normally, gold inflows would have increased reserves, causing commercial banks to expand the money supply by increasing loans to firms and households. However, the Federal Reserve counteracted this monetary expansion by selling government bonds. Economist Richard H. Timberlake lamented, "The commercial banking system would have had $1.05 billion more in reserve assets for its own production of loans and deposits if the Federal Reserve had not existed."[6]

Moreover, the Federal Reserve abdicated its roles as lender of last resort. Instead of extending loans to troubled commercial banks to check runs and prevent financial contagion, the Federal Reserve largely shut its discount window. Through three rounds of bank failures in October 1930, March 1931, and March 1933, the Federal Reserve's loans to commercial banks fell from $1.29 billion in 1928 to $0.12 billion in 1933.

Rather than press the Federal Reserve to act as lender of last resort, Hoover established a new federal agency to perform this function. On January 22, 1932, Hoover signed a law creating the Reconstruction Finance Corporation (RFC) to lend to commercial banks, non-financial corporations, and state and local governments.[7] Given the bureaucratic hurdles in establishing a new agency, the RFC was still not fully functioning when Hoover left office in March 1933.

CORPORATISM

As Secretary of Commerce under both Harding and Coolidge, Hoover had explicitly rejected free market economic policies in favor of a form of corporatism that he called "associationalism." Applying the principles of scientific management originated by Frederick Taylor, Hoover sought to eliminate "wasteful" competition in key industries through price fixing and the division of markets among competing firms. Following the popping of the stock bubble, Hoover attempted to implement associationalism throughout the U.S. economy.

Believing that high wages were the cause rather than the result of American prosperity, Hoover pressed major corporations to maintain their existing levels of production, employment, and compensation. While these corporations attempted to fulfill their pledges to Hoover, weakening demand eventually forced these corporations to reduce their output, lay-off employees, and slash wages.

PROTECTIONISM

During World War I, President Woodrow Wilson appointed Herbert Hoover as Food Administrator. To feed both Allied armies and civilians in Europe, Hoover pressed U.S. farmers to bring marginal lands into production. However, Hoover did not have a postwar plan to take these marginal lands out of production. The combination of (1) global overproduction (as European farmers resumed normal production after the Armistice), (2) an increase in the availability of grain production for human consumption (as farmers substituted motorized equipment for draft animals), and (3) a reduction in demand (because of 20 million war-related deaths) caused agricultural commodity prices to collapse.

By 1928, Hoover realized that his actions as Food Administrator had contributed to a depression in the U.S. agricultural sector. Seeking some way to help farmers, Hoover pressed for higher tariffs on agricultural imports when Congress convened in December 1929. Despite an open letter in the *New York Times* signed by more than one thousand economists (including Irving Fisher, Frank Taussig, Paul Douglas, J. Lawrence Laughlin, and Clair Wilcox) urging a veto,[8] Hoover defiantly signed the *Smoot-Hawley Tariff Act* on June 17, 1930. This act raised U.S. tariff rates on dutiable imports to their highest level in history.

As these economists had predicted, other countries retaliated by raising their tariffs on U.S. exports. Consequently, world trade flows collapsed. U.S. goods imports declined from $5.3 billion in 1929 to just $1.7 billion in 1933, while U.S. goods exports fell from $4.4 billion in 1929 to a mere $1.5 billion in 1933.

COLLAPSE OF THE INTERNATIONAL FINANCIAL SYSTEM DUE TO THE PURSUIT OF INCOMPATIBLE POLICY OBJECTIVES

Free trade was one of the Fourteen Points that President Woodrow Wilson had offered as the basis for a peace settlement of World War I.[9] At the Paris Peace

Conference, however, Wilson (1) sacrificed free trade and (2) acquiesced to vindictive reparations on Germany that were set at $33.4 billion[10] to (1) win approval for his proposal to create a League of Nations and (2) block a Japanese proposal to guarantee racial equality in all signatory countries.[11]

France, the United Kingdom, and other allies expected to repay the $10.4 billion that they had borrowed from the United States during the war with German reparations. To pay these reparations, Germany needed to increase its export earnings substantially above their pre-war level. For German exports to increase sufficiently, the United States and the allies needed to reduce their tariffs. Instead of lowering trade barriers, however, the United States boosted its tariffs in 1922,[12] and other countries retaliated by hiking their tariffs. With insufficient export earnings, Germany became dangerously dependent on investment and loans from the United States to pay reparations.

Hoover did not understand that protectionism, allied repayment of U.S. loans, and German reparations were incompatible policy objectives. As both Secretary of Commerce and President, Hoover saw these issues in moral terms rather than economic terms. On one hand, Hoover was willing to reduce German reparations to the allies because reparations violated his sense of forgiveness and generosity toward the vanquished Germans. On the other, Hoover was unwilling to forgive U.S. loans to the victorious allies because he thought that the allies were financially able and thus had a moral obligation to repay their loans.

After Germany failed to pay a scheduled payment in January 1923, Belgium and France occupied the industrial area of the Ruhr valley. A crisis ensued. France refused to reduce German reparations, while U.S. banks refused to extend new loans to Germany until France agreed to a reduction. U.S. Representative on the Allied Reparations Commission Charles Dawes proposed a plan that was adopted in August 1924. Under the Dawes plan, (1) Belgium and France evacuated their troops from the Ruhr valley; (2) Germany resumed reparations payments, but the amount was temporarily reduced; and (3) U.S. banks resumed making loans to Germany.

By the time Hoover was inaugurated on March 4, 1929, Germany could not meet its escalating reparations payments under the Dawes plan. U.S. from a range of 1.125 percent to 25 percent to a Representative on the Allied Reparations Commission Owen D. Young proposed reducing German reparations. Adopted at the Hague Conference in January 1930, the Young plan (1) limited annual reparations payments to $473 million, two-thirds of which could be postponed, and (2) reduced total reparations payments from $33.4 billion to $26.3 billion.

Deteriorating economic conditions forced Germany to default in early 1931. In response, Hoover arranged a one-year moratorium that began in July 1931. At the Lausanne Conference in July 1932, representatives of allies and Germany finally agreed to a plan that would forgive German reparations if the United States would forgive its loans to the allies. Outraged by the loan forgiveness, Hoover denounced this plan as "a combination" against the American people. He scuttled the plan and refused to extend the moratorium. With Germany unable to pay further reparations, France defaulted on its U.S. loans. Consequently, the international financial system collapsed.[13]

Record Peacetime Increase in Spending

Hoover sought to put the unemployed back to work through federal outlays on public works projects (e.g., Hoover Dam). As a result, federal outlays rose from $3.3 billion (equal to 3.4 percent of GDP) in fiscal year 1930 to $4.6 billion (equal to 8.0 percent of GDP) in fiscal year 1933. As a percent of GDP, Hoover's 4.6 percentage point jump in federal outlays was the largest peacetime increase in federal spending under any president in U.S. history. Indeed, federal outlays were only 2.7 percentage points of GDP higher in their peak fiscal year before the outbreak of World War II under Franklin D. Roosevelt.[14]

The pump-priming spending programs (e.g., Public Works Administration and Works Progress Administration) that Americans associate with Franklin D. Roosevelt's New Deal were actually a politically clever repackaging of Hoover's initiatives. During a moment of unusual candor in a 1974 interview, FDR's economic adviser Rexford Tugwell admitted "practically the whole New Deal was extrapolated from programs Hoover started."[15]

Higher Tax Rates

Immediately after the stock bubble popped, Hoover won approval for a one-year reduction in individual and corporate income tax rates for 1929. Individual rates were reduced range of 0.375 percent on taxable income over $4,000 ($40,000 in 2000 dollars) to 24 percent on taxable income above $100,000 ($1,005,000 in 2000 dollars), while the corporate rate fell from 12 percent to 11 percent.

Prior the institution of withholding and estimated tax payments under the *Current Tax Payment Act* in 1943, federal taxes owed on income earned in one year were paid by taxpayers in quarterly installments during the following year (i.e., taxpayers paid federal taxes owed on income earned in 1929 in quarterly installments during 1930). Thus, the economic effects of Hoover's one- year rate reduction for 1929 were similar to a one- off tax rebate under the current tax system.

While Hoover's one-year reduction in income tax rates for 1929 improved the cash flow of households and firms in 1930, Hoover's reduction did not provide any stimulus to increase production and investment because households and firms could not retroactively change the economic decisions that they had made during 1929. At most, Hoover's one-year rate reduction for 1929 provided a modest boost to consumption in 1930.[16]

Collapsing tax revenues and Hoover's spending initiatives produced large federal budget deficits. The federal government moved from a surplus of $734 million (equal to 0.8 percent of GDP) in fiscal year 1930 to a deficit of $2.6 billion (equal to 4.5 percent of GDP) in fiscal year 1933.

Opposed to budget deficits largely on moral grounds, Hoover pressed Congress to enact the largest tax increase in U.S. history up to that time in a vain attempt to balance the budget. Once again, Hoover blithely disregarded warnings from his friend, John Maynard Keynes, and other prominent economists not to increase taxes.

The *Revenue Act of 1932* hiked individual income tax rates to a range of 4 percent on taxable incomes over $4,000 ($50,430 in 2000 dollars) to 63 percent on taxable income over $1,000,000 ($12,610,000 in 2000 dollars). The corporate tax rate rose from 12 percent to 15 percent. Estate tax rates jumped from a range of 1 percent to 20 percent to a range of 1 percent to 40 percent on taxable estates above $10,000,000 ($126,100,000 in 2000 dollars). The gift tax was re-instated, and depositors paid a two-cent excise tax on every check written.

Prior to passage, the Treasury estimated that the 1932 act would produce additional revenue of $1.1 billion. This estimate proved wildly optimistic. Instead, tax revenues actually rose only by $43 million from fiscal year 1932 to fiscal year 1933.

Conclusion

Hoover did not understand the monetary causes for the stock market bubble, its popping, and the subsequent contraction in U.S. output and prices. Nor did Hoover appreciate how international imbalances spread the worsening economic contraction around the world. Repeatedly ignoring the sound advice of prominent economists, Hoover actively pursued bad economic policies based on his wrong-headed notions, his quirky morality, and his anti-bank, anti-Wall Street prejudices that deepened and lengthened the Great Depression.

End Notes

[1] Milton Friedman and Anna Jacobson Schwartz, *A Monetary History of the United States, 1967-1960* (Princeton, NJ: Princeton University Press, 1963).

[2] Among the remaining five members, Hoover appointed Eugene Meyer as Chairman in 1930 and Wayland Magee in 1931 and reappointed George Jones in 1931.

[3] The real bills doctrine of monetary policy holds that central banks should increase or decrease the money supply in proportion to the extension of short-term loans by commercial banks to non-financial firms that (1) are used to finance the production of goods and services and (2) are repaid from the sale of such goods and services. In the 19th century, these loans were known as "real bills," hence the name of this doctrine. The real bills doctrine is pro-cyclical, directing a central bank to expand the monetary supply during economic upswings and to contract it during downswings.

[4] Walter Bagehot, *Lombard Street: A Description of the Money Market* (Homewood, IL: R. D. Irwin, 1963 [1873]).

[5] The United Kingdom abandoned the gold standard on September 20, 1931. Other countries soon followed. By 1932, the fear that the United States would also abandon the gold standard caused the gold flow to reverse from an inflow to an outflow.

[6] Richard H. Timberlake, *Monetary Policy in the United States: An Intellectual History* (Chicago: University of Chicago Press, 1993), 226.

[7] Ironically, Federal Reserve Chairman Eugene Meyer, who had presided over the Federal Reserve's failure to perform its lender of last resort function, urged Hoover to sign the bill establishing the RFC as an alternative lender of last resort. Had Meyer directed the Federal Reserve to perform the lender of last resort function for which it had been established, the RFC would have been superfluous.

[8] "1,028 Economists Ask Hoover To Veto Pending Tariff Bill," *The New York Times* (May 4, 1930), 1. Found at:
http://www.clubforgrowth.org/media/uploads/smooth%20hawley%20ny%20times%2005%2005%2030.pdf.

[9] "III. The removal, so far as possible, of all economic barriers and the establishment of an equality of trade conditions among all the nations consenting to the peace and associating themselves for its maintenance." Woodrow Wilson, *Address to a Joint Session of Congress*, 65th Cong., 2nd sess. (January 8, 1918). For text, see: http://www.yale.edu/lawweb/avalon/wilson14.htm.

[10] This amount was fixed by the Allied Reparations Commission in 1921.

[11] If Japan had prevailed, the *Treaty of Versailles* would have effectively outlawed the policy of racial segregation that Wilson had promoted in the United States.

[12] On September 21, 1922, Harding signed the *FordneyMcCumber Tariff Act*, which boosted the average tariff rate on dutiable imports from 27 percent to 38.5 percent.

[13] Ron Chernow, *The House of Morgan: An American Banking Dynasty and the Rise of Modern Finance* (New York: Grove Press, 2001), 350-351.

[14] Federal outlays were $6.5 billion (equal to 10.7 percent of GDP) in fiscal year 1934. Federal outlays remained at or below 10.7 percent of GDP through fiscal year 1940.

[15] See: http://www.pbs.org/wgbh/amex/goldengate/sfeature/sf_3 0s.html .

[16] Prior to 1943, an income tax rate reduction would have had to have been in effect for at least two years to have an incentive effect on production and investment.

In: Economic Crises as a Result of Distrust ISBN: 978-1-60741-355-4
Editors: Emilio Gullini

Chapter 8

HOUSING BUBBLE AND THE GLOBAL FINANCIAL CRISIS

Jim Saxton

An unprecedented U.S. housing bubble began to inflate in the first quarter of 1998 and then popped in the second quarter of 2006. The subsequent deflation of housing prices has caused the delinquency and foreclosure rates for subprime residential mortgage loans to soar. Investors grew uncertain about the value of the residential mortgage-backed securities (RMBS) and the collateralized mortgage obligations (CMOs) into which many subprime residential mortgage loans had been placed. Consequently, the market liquidity for these subprime-related derivative securities shriveled.

KINDLEBERGER ASSET BUBBLE FRAMEWORK

After reviewing all asset bubbles from 1720 to 1999, economist Charles P. Kindleberger devised a seven- stage framework of assets bubbles.[1] The stages are:

1. Displacement of existing expectations
2. Credit expansion
3. Proclamation of a new economy
4. Swindles
5. Overtrading, revulsion, and discredit
6. Financial panic and crisis management

7. Aftermath

This framework provides an analytical tool for understanding the U.S. housing bubble and the resulting global financial crisis. This chapter examines stages one, two (monetary policy and other macro-economic factors), three, four, and five as they apply to the U.S. housing bubble. Future reports will investigate stages two (micro-economic factors related to financial services), six, and seven.

DISPLACEMENT OF EXISTING EXPECTATIONS

The Great Moderation, which refers to the combination of long and strong expansions, short and shallow recessions, and low inflation since 1983, increased the propensity for risk-taking throughout the U.S. economy. After the high-tech stock bubble popped in the first quarter of 2000, many Americans saw housing as a "safe" alternative that could still produce a high rate of return.

Housing prices began their rapid ascent in the first quarter of 1998. From then until the peak of the housing bubble in the second quarter of 2006, U.S. housing prices jumped by 101 percent (or 80 percent after adjusting for inflation).[2] U.S. housing prices deviated from their long-established relationships with household income and changes in rental costs.

Over the long term, housing demand is a function of household formation and household income growth. The ratio of the median sales price of an existing single-family house to the median household income averaged 3.19 from 1969 to 1997, but increased to 4.69 in 2005.[3]

Over the long term, housing prices closely track changes in the rental costs for apartments. From 1998 to 2006, however, the median sales price of an existing single-family house ballooned by an average of 6.3 percent a year, while rental costs increased by an average of 3.4 percent a year.[4]

CREDIT EXPANSION

During the last decade, the credit available to U.S. households and non-financial firms grew much faster than GDP. Total credit outstanding including total debt securities outstanding in U.S. credit markets and total loans and leases outstanding at U.S. depository institutions grew from $17.087 trillion (equal to

205.8 percent of GDP) on December 31, 1997 to $38.324 trillion (equal to 276.8 percent of GDP) on December 31, 2007.[5]

This chapter examines the monetary policy and macro-economic supply factors in U.S. credit markets that contributed to the credit expansion. Micro-economic factors relating to financial services will be discussed in a later report.

Economist John B. Taylor developed the widely respected Taylor rule to guide the Federal Reserve on how to change its target for the federal funds rate to maintain price stability while maximize long-term real GDP growth. Comparing actual data with data from a Taylor rule-consistent simulation, Taylor (2007) found that the actual federal funds rate was significantly below the Taylor rule-consistent target federal funds rate from the second quarter of 2002 through the third quarter of 2006. He concluded that "a higher federal funds rate path (consistent with the Taylor rule) would have avoided much of the housing boom."[6]

Monetary policy-induced low short-term U.S. interest rates decreased the cost of funds for banks, other depository institutions, and highly leveraged non-depository financial institutions.[7] In turn, low funding costs encouraged financial institutions to expand credit aggressively by extending loans and purchasing debt and derivative securities.

At the same time, two macro-economic supply factors in U.S. credit markets restrained medium- and long-term U.S. interest rates:

- Globalization greatly intensified price competition among tradable goods and services in the United States. The inflation-suppressing effects of globalization on goods and services prices as recorded by the Consumer Price Index (CPI), the GDP Deflator, and the Personal Consumption Expenditure (PCE) Deflator combined with the Federal Reserve's successful disinflationary monetary policy during the 1980s and early 1990s to foster stable inflationary expectations. This discouraged U.S. lenders from seeking high inflation premiums in medium- and long-term interest rates when monetary policy deviated from the Taylor rule.
- Since the Asian Financial Crisis of 1997-98, the People's Republic of China (PRC) has intervened heavily in foreign exchange markets to maintain a fixed exchange rate between the Chinese renminbi and the U.S. dollar through July 20, 2005 and to suppress the appreciation of the renminbi relative to the dollar thereafter. Other Asian governments mimicked the PRC's foreign exchange policy to maintain the price competitiveness of their manufactured exports with China's. By buying U.S. dollars and selling their currencies simultaneously, central banks in

> the PRC, India, Indonesia, Japan, Malaysia, South Korea, Taiwan, and Thailand added $2.06 trillion to their foreign exchange reserves from December 31, 1997 to the peak of the U.S. housing bubble on June 30, 2006. About 2/3 of these newly acquired foreign exchange reserves were invested in U.S. dollar- denominated debt securities, mainly U.S. Treasuries and U.S. Agencies.[8] Massive purchases by these central banks bid-up the prices of U.S. debt securities and consequently held down medium- and long-term U.S. interest rates.

Housing is the most interest rate-sensitive sector of the U.S. economy. Low long-term U.S. interest rates during the first half of this decade further stimulated the already strong demand for housing among households, while financial institutions enthusiastically supplied the necessary residential mortgage credit. Thus, an overly accommodative monetary policy and macroeconomic supply factors in U.S. credit markets fueled a massive credit expansion that helped to inflate an unsustainable bubble in U.S. housing prices.

New Economy

Both major political parties have promoted home ownership among financially marginal and minority households. The Clinton administration pressed depository institutions and mortgage banks to lower their credit standards and reduce down payment requirements. It also promoted exotic alternatives to traditional fixed-rate fully amortizing residential mortgage loans, such as interest-only residential mortgage loans and negatively amortizing residential mortgage loans. These policies were intended to help financially marginal and minority households that could not qualify for traditional residential mortgage loans under normal credit standards to buy homes and thereby to increase the home ownership rate. The Bush administration did not change these policies.

Under provisions of the GSE Act, the Department of Housing and Urban Development has issued three sets of progressively more ambitious affordable housing regulations for Fannie Mae and Freddie Mac: December 1, 1995 for the years 1996-2000; October 31, 2000 for the years 2001-2004; and November 2, 2004 for the years 2005-2008.[9]

Before the 2000 regulations, Fannie Mae and Freddie Mac purchased relatively few subprime residential mortgage loans for securitization. To meet their more ambitious affordable housing goals under the 2000 regulations, Fannie Mae and Freddie Mac stepped-up their purchases of the AAA-rated subprime-related RMBS and tranches of subprimerelated CMOs issued by investment banks. By increasing the demand for subprime-related RMBS and subprime-related tranches of CMOs, Fannie Mae and Freddie Mac unwittingly encouraged the origination of subprime residential mortgage loans by mortgage banks and accelerated the private issuance of subprime-related RMBS and subprimerelated CMOs by investment banks.

Collectively, these federal policies encouraged many financially marginal and minority households to buy homes during the bubble. The home ownership rate, which had averaged 64.3 percent of all households from 1982 to 1997, climbed to a peak of 69.0 percent in 2004.[10] As early as 2000, economist Robert Shiller voiced warnings about the inflation of an unsustainable housing bubble.

Moreover, an explosion of television shows and even entire cable networks (e.g., *Flip This House* and *Sell This House* on A&E, *Flip That House* on the Learning Channel, and the Home and Garden Network) promoted home-buying, remodeling, and speculation in housing. This convinced many households that:

- Housing was a "safe" investment because housing prices never go down;
- Leverage increased the potential for high rates of return;
- Households could safely stretch their finances to buy or remodel housing; and
- "Flipping" was a good strategy to make money.

SWINDLES

Not surprisingly, swindlers took advantage of the unsuspecting during the housing bubble. The swindles included:

- Households that misrepresented their financial condition or committed other frauds to qualify for residential mortgage loans;
- Mortgage bankers that knowingly extended residential mortgage loans to unqualified households because securitization transferred the likely losses from poor credit standards and risky underwriting practices to the buyers of the derivative securities into which these loans were placed;
- Mortgage bankers that earned higher fees from issuers by pushing households that could qualify for prime residential mortgage loans to take out subprime residential mortgage loans instead; and

- Home builders and realtors that boosted their sales by encouraging households to take out subprime residential mortgage loans to speculate on housing units.

Overtrading, Revulsion, and Discredit

Since the 1930s, financially marginal households that could not qualify for prime residential mortgage loans – due to their inability to make a substantial down-payment, their high debt service-to-income ratios, their limited net worth, or their poor credit histories – have obtained insured residential mortgage loans through the Federal Housing Administration (FHA) program. During the housing bubble, the overall share of residential mortgage loans going to financially marginal households remained stable. However, the market share of private subprime residential mortgage loans grew from 3.8 percent of all residential mortgage loans serviced in the fourth quarter of 2002 to a peak of 14.0 percent in the second quarter of 2007 before falling to 12.7 percent in fourth quarter of 2007, while the FHA market share fell from 20.8 percent in the first quarter of 1998 to a trough of 6.9 percent in the fourth quarter of 2007.[11]

To qualify as many financially marginal households as possible, mortgage bankers promoted adjustable-rate subprime mortgage loans with "teaser" provisions to reduce initial monthly payments. Teasers included periods of low fixed interest rates, interest-only payments, or negative amortization. Adjustable-rate subprime residential mortgage loans increased from 20.6 percent of all subprime residential mortgage loans serviced in the first quarter of 1998 to 50.4 percent at the peak of the housing bubble in the second quarter of 2006.[12] As a result, interest rate risk became concentrated among financially marginal households that were least able to shoulder it.

Before housing prices peaked, subprime borrowers could generally sell their homes at a profit or refinance them with another mortgage loan before their interest rate adjusted and their monthly payments increased. Essentially, both subprime borrowers and their creditors relied on ever increasing housing prices rather than the borrower's income to repay subprime mortgage loans.

After the peak, this was no longer possible. When the initial teasers expired, interest rates increased, monthly payments spiked, and the delinquency and foreclosure rates for subprime residential mortgage loans soared. From the fourth quarter of 2004 to fourth quarter of 2007, the delinquency rate for adjustable-rate subprime residential mortgage loans exploded from 9.83 percent to 20.02 percent, while the delinquency rate for fixed-rate subprime residential mortgage loans rose from 9.72 percent to 13.99 percent.[13]

The foreclosure initiation rate on fixed-rate subprime borrowers increased from 1.05 percent in the fourth quarter of 2005 to 1.52 percent in the fourth quarter of 2007. More ominously, the foreclosure initiation rate for adjustable rate subprime borrowers jumped from 1.55 percent in the fourth quarter of 2005 to 5.29 percent in the fourth quarter of 2007.[14]

EXTENT OF THE FALLOUT

Greenlaw et al. (2008) used a variety of methods to estimate the global credit losses from subprime mortgage loans, subprime-related RMBS, and tranches of subprime-related CDOs. The authors projected that global subprime-related credit losses will be $400 billion.[15] The OECD (2008) used a default loss model to estimate global subprime-related credit losses. Assuming a 40 percent recovery, the OECD forecast global subprime mortgage-related credit losses will be $422 billion.[16]

The estimates from the Greenlaw et al. and OECD studies include only subprime-related credit losses. The IMF (2008 A), which does not break out subprime-related credit losses, forecasts the global credit losses of $565 billion from all residential mortgage loans and related securities.[17]

As housing prices neared their top, sales of new single-family homes peaked at a seasonally adjusted annual rate of 1.389 million in July 2005 and have subsequently fallen by 62.1 percent to a seasonally adjusted annual rate of 526,000 in March 2008.[18] Existing single-family home sales peaked at a seasonally adjusted annual rate of 6.340 million in September 2005 and have subsequently fallen by 31.4 percent to a seasonally adjusted annual rate of 4.350 million in March 2008.[19]

New housing starts also peaked at a seasonally adjusted annual rate of 2.273 million in January 2006 and have subsequently fallen by 58.0 percent to a seasonally adjusted annual rate of 954,000 in March 2008.[20] As a result, payroll employment in residential construction and related specialty trades peaked at 3.444 million in March 2006 and has subsequently fallen by 13.6 percent to 2.977 million in April 2008.[21]

During 2007, at least twenty-five mortgage bankers that had specialized in originating subprime mortgage loans filed for bankruptcy. On April 2, 2007, New Century Financial, reportedly the largest mortgage banker that had specialized in originating subprime residential mortgage loans, filed for bankruptcy.

However, failures and near failures among mortgage banks were not confined to those that specialized in the subprime segment. American Home Mortgage Investment Corporation, the tenth largest mortgage bank with a 3 percent share of the origination market, filed for bankruptcy on August 6, 2007. Soon afterwards, Countrywide Financial, which operated the largest mortgage bank with a 17 percent share of the origination market, a federal savings bank, an investment bank affiliate (which is a primary dealer),[22] and insurance affiliate, came under extreme financial stress as a run began on its savings bank. On August 16, 2007, Countrywide narrowly avoid bankruptcy after securing an emergency $11.5 billion line of credit from a consortium of forty commercial banks. On January 11, 2008, Bank of America agreed to buy Countrywide for $4.1 billion, about one-sixth of its market value one year earlier.

CONCLUSION

This chapter examined the causes of the U.S. housing bubble and the economic stress that the popping and deflation of this bubble has inflicted upon the housing sector and housing- related finance. Weakness in the U.S. housing sector ignited a global financial crisis on August 9, 2007, that will be explored in a future report. The IMF (2008 A) estimates the global credit losses from the financial crisis will be $945 billion.[23] The IMF (2008 B) forecasts that the U.S. housing prices will fall another 12 percent in 2008.[24] The IMF (2008 B) concluded that the combination of the aftermath of the housing bubble and the credit crunch arising from the global financial crisis has tipped the U.S. economy into a recession.[25] Whether or not this IMF forecast proves correct, economic growth in the United States slowed dramatically during the last the two quarters.

End Notes

[1] See generally, Charles P. Kindleberger, *Manias, Panics, and Crashes: A History of Financial Crises* (1978; 4th ed., New York: John Wiley & Sons, 2000).

[2] S&P/Case-Shiller Home Price Index: U.S. National/Haver and Consumer Price Index-U: All Items/Bureau of Labor Statistics/Haver. Author calculated real index by adjusting nominal index by CPI. Author calculated percentage changes.

[3] Median Sales Price: Existing Single-Family Homes, United States (Current Dollars)/National Association of Realtors/Haver and Median Income of Households (Current Dollars)/Census Bureau/Haver. Author calculated ratios and standard deviations. N.B., 2006 is the latest year in which annual household income data are available.

[4] Consumer Price Index-U: Rent of Primary Residence, Percent Change - Year to Year/Bureau of Labor Statistics/Haver and Median Sales Price: Existing Single- Family Homes, United States (Current Dollars) Percent Change - Year to Year/National Association of Realtors/Haver.

[5] Credit market data are from U.S. Department of Treasury, Federal Reserve System, Federal Agencies, Thomson Financial, Bloomberg, Securities Industry and Financial Market Association estimates. Nominal GDP data are from Bureau of Economic Analysis. Author calculated credit market data as a percent of GDP.

[6] John B. Taylor, "Housing and Monetary Policy," Presentation to Jackson Hole Conference (September 2007). Found at http://www.stanford.edu/~johntayl/Housing%20and%20Monetary%20Policy--Taylor--Jackson%20Hole%202007.pdf.

[7] Highly leveraged non-depository financial institutions (HLNDFIs) are discussed in detail in a later report. HLNDFIs include finance companies, financial government-sponsored enterprises (GSEs), hedge funds, investment banks, and bank-sponsored off-balance sheet entities (OBSEs).

[8] For an extensive discussion, see: Robert P. O'Quinn, *Chinese FX Interventions Caused International Imbalances, Contributed To U.S. Housing Bubble* (Prepared for Joint Economic Committee, 110th Cong., 2nd sess., March 2008). Found at: http://www.house.gov/jec/studies/2008/Chinese%20FX %20Interventions%20Caused% 20International%20Imbalances%20Contributed%20to%20U%20S%20%20Housing% 20Bubble%20(2).pdf.

[9] Fannie Mae is commonly used name for the Federal National Mortgage Association, and Freddie Mac is the commonly used name for the Federal Home Loan Mortgage Corporation.

[10] Census Bureau/Haver.

[11] Mortgage Bankers Association/Haver.

[12] Mortgage Bankers Association/Haver.

[13] Mortgage Bankers Association/Haver.

[14] Mortgage Bankers Association/Haver.

[15] David Greenlaw, Jan Hatzius, Anil K. Kashyap, and Hyun Song Shin, *Leveraged Losses: Lessons from the Mortgage Market Meltdown*, Presented at the U.S. Monetary Policy Forum Conference (February 29, 2008).

[16] *The Subprime Crisis: Size, Deleveraging, and Some Policy Options* (Paris: Organization for Economic Cooperation and Development, April 2008), pp. 7-11.

[17] *World Economic and Financial Surveys, Global Financial Stability Report: Containing Systemic Risk and Restoring Financial Soundness* (Washington, D.C.: International Monetary Fund, April 2008), pg. 50.

[18] Census Bureau/Haver. Author calculated percent change.

[19] National Association of Realtors/Haver. Author calculated percent change.

[20] Census Bureau/Haver. Author calculated percent change.

[21] Bureau of Labor Statistics/Haver. Author calculated percent change.

[22] A primary dealer is a bank or securities broker-dealer that may trade directly with the Federal Reserve. A primary dealer is required to make bids or offers when the Federal Reserve conducts open market operations, provide information to the Federal Reserve's trading desk, and to participate actively in Treasury auctions.

[23] *Global Financial Stability Report* (2008), pg. 10.

[24] *World Economic and Financial Surveys, World Economic Outlook: Housing and the Business Cycle* (Washington, D.C.: International Monetary Fund, April 2008), pg. 68. Author subtracted the decline in the S&P/Case-Shiller Index in 2006 and 2007 from the IMF forecast for the peak to year-end 2008 decline in this index to isolate the decline in 2008.

[25] *World Economic Outlook* (April 2008), pg. 65.

In: Economic Crises as a Result of Distrust
Editors: Emilio Gullini
ISBN: 978-1-60741-355-4

Chapter 9

HOUSING BUBBLE AND THE GLOBAL FINANCIAL CRISIS - VULNERABILITIES

Jim Saxton

INTRODUCTION

This chapter explains how weakness in the U.S. housing sector morphed into a global financial crisis that began last August. Using the framework for analyzing asset bubbles that was introduced in a previous report,[1] this chapter examines stage two – credit expansion (microeconomic factors related to financial services) and stage six – financial panic and crisis management.[2]

ALTERNATIVE FINANCIAL SYSTEM

During the last three decades, an alternative financial system evolved to the traditional bank-centric system that had characterized developed economies since the Renaissance. This alternative financial system is based on **structured finance**.[3]

The most common form of structured finance is the **securitization** of loans, leases, and receivables from households and non-financial firms that cannot access credit markets directly by issuing debt securities. **Originators** extend loans, leases, and receivables to households and non-financial firms. **Issuers** buy these loans, leases, and receivables, place them as collateral into

special purpose vehicles (SPVs) that are legally separate from the issuer, and sell **derivative securities** in the SPVs. This "securitizes" the collateral.

When derivative securities in a SPV have *equal and undifferentiated* interests in the cash flow from the underlying collateral, such securities are known as **asset-backed securities (ABS)**, or **residential mortgage-backed securities (RMBS)** when the collateral consists of residential mortgage loans.

Alternatively, when SPVs are divided into tranches of derivative securities that have *unequal and differentiated* interests in the cash flow from the underlying collateral, such securities are known as **collateralized debt obligations (CDOs)**, or **collateralized mortgage obligations (CMOs)** when the collateral consists of residential mortgage loans.

Highly Leveraged Non-depository Financial Institutions

Highly leveraged non-depository financial institutions (HLNDFIs) include **finance companies**,[4] **financial government-sponsored enterprises (GSEs)**,[5] **hedge funds**,[6] **investment banks**,[7] and **bank-sponsored off-balance sheet entities (OBSEs)**.[8] In general, these institutions "borrow short" through commercial paper, repurchase agreements (repos), reserve repurchase agreements (reverse repos), and other debt securities to "lend long" by investing in medium- and long-term debt and derivative securities, many of which have limited market liquidity.[9] Many of these institutions make their funding and investment decisions based on complex mathematical models that try to discern predictable relations between various prices, different interest rates, and other market indicators. Unfortunately, these relations often break down under extreme conditions in financial markets.

Since 1980, this alternative financial system has grown rapidly to rival the bank-centric system. In 2007, the $12.7 trillion of U.S. financial assets held by HLNDFIs almost equaled the $13.5 trillion held by depository institutions.[10]

In general, HLNDFIs have significantly higher leverage ratios (i.e., debt and other liabilities to equity) than banks and other depository institutions. Graph 1 compares the leverage ratios of the four largest finance companies, the four largest independent investment banks, and the three largest financial GSEs with the average leverage ratio at all U.S. banks and savings institutions.[11] Of course, high leverage ratios simultaneously increase both potential returns and credit risk in HLNDFIs.

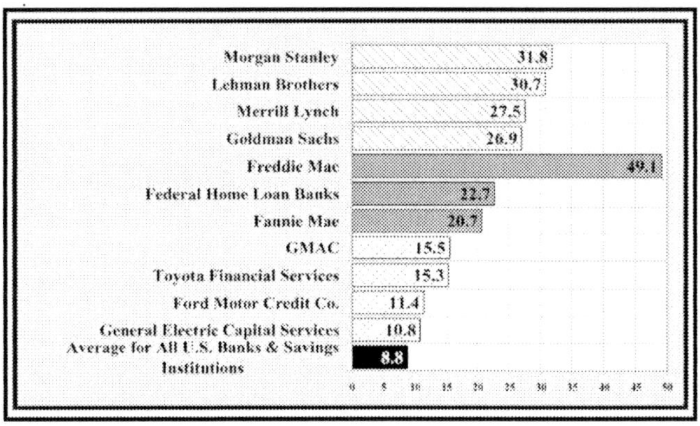

Graph 1. Leverage Ratios at Major Highly Leveraged Financial Institutions by Type (End of First Financial Quarter 2008)

Intermediation and Liquidity and Maturity Transformation

HLNDFIs are now performing the same economically vital, but inherently risky functions of **intermediation** and **liquidity and maturity transformation**, which banks and other depository institutions have traditionally performed. During the 19th and early 20th centuries, largely unregulated and unsupervised banks and other depository institutions were frequently subject to runs (i.e., the simultaneous demand from a large number of depositors to convert their deposits into cash). Bank runs often became contagious, triggering financial panics that were characterized by asset price declines, credit contractions, bank failures, and financial stress among households and non-financial firms. Financial panics usually caused recessions or even depressions. Bitter experience taught policymakers in the United States and other developed economies that the banking system requires an appropriate regulatory and supervisory framework, including:

- **Capital adequacy regulation** (i.e., a minimum capital ratio, defined as equity plus certain reserves to assets) that caps the leverage in banks and other depository institutions;[12]

- **Central banks** that serve as "lenders of the last resort" to illiquid, but solvent banks and other depository institutions in order to check contagious bank runs and to prevent widespread financial panics and the resulting damage to the economy;

- **Deposit insurance** that prevents runs by guaranteeing depositors against losses if their bank or other depository institution should fail; and

- **Prudential supervision** that detects fraud and other misconduct in banks and other depository institutions, monitors their financial condition, and provides an early warning system for institution-specific or systemic financial problems so that central banks, regulators, and finance ministries can take corrective actions before financial crises develop.

Microeconomic Factors – Regulation and Supervision

Two regulatory and supervisory factors contributed to the credit expansion that inflated an unsustainable housing bubble in the United States:

- **Inherent limitations in value-at-risk models used to assess credit, market and operational risk exposure**. Large banks, HLNDFIs, and regulators use these models to estimate credit, market, and operational risks and to determine the capital adequacy given these risks at banks, other depository institutions, and HLNDFIs. The lack of sufficient performance data for new financial products especially under stressful market conditions caused value-at-risk models to underestimate risk exposure. Consequently, banks, other depository institutions, and HLNDFIs continued to fund the rapid expansion of residential mortgage credit long after it should have been curtailed.

- **Failure to incorporate off-balance sheet entities within the regulatory perimeter**. Bank regulators failed to include bank-sponsored off-balance sheet entities within the regulatory perimeter for assessing capital adequacy. Banks sponsored these entities to reduce costs and increase profits by circumventing capital regulations and employing higher leverage. These entities allowed banks to disguise their actual leverage and their potential exposure to credit, liquidity, and market risk. When these entities suffered from funding illiquidity, this risk exposure was actualized.

Two regulatory and supervisory factors contributed to the resulting global financial crisis after the U.S. housing bubble popped:

- **Fragmentation.**The regulation and supervision of financial services firms is highly fragmented among eight federal agencies[13] and the states[14] and does not reflect the rise of the alternative financial system and its integration with the bank-centric system. Because of the lack of prudential supervision of highly leveraged non-depository financial institutions, the Federal Reserve and other central banks were surprised by large funding liquidity problems among these institutions. The Federal Reserve was forced to act as the lender of the last resort to these institutions to check financial contagion once the crisis began.

- **Mark-to-market accounting for level three assets**. Under generally accepted accounting principles, fair value accounting (often called mark-to-market accounting) requires financial institutions to use (1) market prices to value liquid financial assets (referred to as level one or level two assets) and (2) theoretical models based on price inputs to value illiquid financial assets (referred to as level three assets). Mark-to-market accounting increases transparency in financial institutions, but is also pro-cyclical. Because of the inherent limitations in these theoretical models, mark-to-market accounting may exaggerate the decline in the fair value of level three assets under stressful market conditions. Moreover, mark-to-market accounting forces financial institutions to write-down paper losses on debt and derivative securities that these institutions do not intend to sell, reducing their equity. During the global financial crisis, mark-to-market accounting triggered fire sales of some debt and derivative securities that accelerated their fall in value.

Microeconomic Factors – Private Firms

Three misalignments of private incentives in the alternative financial system as well as one significant methodological error contributed to the credit expansion that inflated the U.S. housing bubble and exacerbated the vulnerability of the alternative financial system to a global crisis:

- The **"originate to securitize"** business model of mortgage banks tempted them to weaken their credit standards for extending loans that were going to be securitized. Originators maximized their income by extending and selling as many loans as possible to issuers, while the credit losses from the neglect of good credit standards accrued to the buyers of derivative securities.
- The **"issuer pays"** business model for credit rating agencies, in which the issuers of debt and derivative securities pay credit rating agencies for their ratings, tempted these agencies to give overly favorable credit ratings to derivative securities to win contracts from major investment banks that were issuing a very large volume of derivative securities.
- **"Up front" incentive compensation plans**, which rewarded investment bankers for the volume of their transactions in a single year rather than the long-term profitability of their transactions for the investment bank or its customers, tempted investment bankers to take excessive risk by underwriting as many debt securities and derivative securities as possible regardless of their long-term profitability.

In addition to these misalignments of private incentives, the both Financial Stability Forum and the IMF found that credit rating agencies employed flawed methodologies in assessing the default risk in derivative securities. Simply put, credit rating agencies systemically underestimated the likelihood that defaults on the underlying collateral would happen at the same time (e.g., declining housing prices would cause many subprime borrowers to become delinquent and default simultaneously). Because of this error, credit rating agencies awarded excessively high credit ratings to many derivative securities.[15]

Ignition of a Financial Panic

After the housing bubble burst in the second quarter of 2006, soaring delinquency and foreclosure rates for subprime residential mortgage loans reduced the market value of subprime-related RMBS and tranches of subprime-related CMOs. Consequently, their market liquidity shriveled.

On August 9, 2007, BNP-Paribas suspended cash redemptions from three hedge funds that it had sponsored because of uncertainty about the value of subprime-related RMBS and tranches of subprimerelated CMOs in these funds. This suspension triggered a severe global financial crisis that has made borrowing more difficult and costly for all but the most creditworthy households and non-financial firms.

Losses in highly rated subprime-related RMBS and tranches of subprime-related CMOs undermined investor confidence in credit ratings and triggered a general reassessment of risk that boosted credit and market liquidity risk premiums across the board.

Real estate loans comprised 60.2 percent of all loans and leases in all U.S. banks and savings institutions on March 31, 2008. Largely because of this concentration, the average seasonally adjusted delinquency rate for loans and leases in U.S. banks jumped from 1.51 percent in the second quarter of 2006 when the housing bubble popped to 2.83 rate for loans and leases in all U.S. banks increased from 0.42 percent in the second quarter of 2006 to 0.97 percent in the first quarter of 2008.[16]

Table 1. Percent of U.S. Banks Reporting a Tightening of Credit Standards in Q1-2008

Commercial & Industrial Loans	
Large Non-Financial Firms	55.5%
Small Non-Financial Firms	51.8%
Commercial Real Estate Loans	78.6%
Prime Residential Mortgage Loans	62.3%
Subprime Residential Mortgage Loans	77.7%
Home Equity Lines of Credit	70.3%
Consumer Installment Loans	44.4%
Credit Cards	32.4%

Source: Federal Reserve Survey of Senior Bank Officers

Banks became uncertain about the credit risk in lending to other banks. This uncertainty increased the spread of the three-month London Interbank Offer Rate (LIBOR) over the effective federal funds rate from 9.0 basis points on August 9, 2007, to 89.5 basis points the next day. This spread has remained high (68.6 basis points on June 6, 2008).

Bank-sponsored off-balance sheet entities that had heavily invested in subprime-related RMBS and tranches of subprime-related CMOs were unable to rollover their asset-backed commercial paper. Thus, asset-backed commercial paper outstanding fell by 38.4 percent from $1.1 95 trillion for the week ending August 8, 2007 to $753 billion for the week ending June 4, 2008.

Because of this funding illiquidity, these off-balance sheet entities drew down their back-up lines of credit with sponsoring banks, and sponsoring banks were forced to absorb OBSE assets onto their balance sheets. This involuntary increase in bank assets, the rapid escalation in charge-offs on subprime residential mortgage loans, mark-tomarket write-downs on subprime-related RMBS and tranches of subprime-related CDOs reduced the regulatory capital ratios at many banks.[17]

In response, banks have tightened their credit standards to strengthen their balance sheets (see Table 1).[18]

As the market value of subprime-related RMBS and tranches of subprime-related CMOs plummeted, banks increased their "haircuts" and made margin calls on lines of credit to highly leveraged non-depository financial institutions especially hedge funds (see Table 2). For example, the amount that such institutions could borrow under lines of credit by pledging Treasuries as collateral fell from 99.75 percent of their value in early 2007 to 97 percent of their market value in April 2008.

Larger haircuts and margin calls on lines of credit reduced the funding liquidity in many HLNDFIs. Some of these institutions dumped some of their debt and derivative securities in "fire sales." Deleveraging increased interest rate spreads for most debt securities over Treasuries with comparable maturities.

Banks and other depository institutions have also increased their interest rate margins on most loans to households and non-financial firms to restore profitability. Consequently, interest rates paid by households and non-financial firms have not generally decreased as the Federal Reserve has reduced the cost of funds for banks and other depository institutions.

Table 2. Typical "Haircut" on Collateral for Lines of Credit to Hedge Funds (in percent)

Security	Jan-May 2007	April 2008
U.S. Treasuries	0.25	3
Investment-grade Bonds	0-3	8-12
Non-investment-grade Bonds	10-15	25-40
Equities	15	20
Investment-grade CDS	1	5
Synthetic-super-senior	1	2
Senior Leveraged Loans	10-12	15-20
Second-lien Leveraged Loans	15-20	25-3 5
Mezzanine Level Loans	18-25	35+
AAA ABS CDOs	2-4	15
AA ABS CDOs	8-15	30-50
A ABS CDOs	8-15	30-50
BBB ABS CDOs	10-20	40-70
Equity ABS CDOs	50	100
AAA CLO	4	10-20
AAA RMBS	2-4	10-20
Alt-a MBS	3-5	20-50

Sources: Citigroup and IMF Staff Estimates

MONETARY RESPONSE

The Federal Reserve has been forced to take extraordinary measures to maintain liquidity and keep credit markets functioning. First, the Federal Reserve has aggressively eased monetary policy. From August 16, 2007 to April 30, 2008, the Federal Reserve reduced its discount rate by 400 basis points from 6.25 percent to 2.25 percent. From September 16, 2007 to April 30, 2008, the Federal Reserve slashed its target federal funds rate by 325 basis points from 5.25 percent to 2.00 percent.

The Federal Reserve has also created new loan programs to alleviate the funding liquidity crisis. To provide more than overnight funding for banks and other depository institutions, the Federal Reserve established the **Term Discount Window Program** on August 17, 2007 through which banks and other depository institutions could borrow on terms similar to the overnight discount window for up to ninety days. After funding liquidity conditions worsened, the Federal Reserve established the **Term Action Facility** on December 12, 2007. Under this facility, banks and other depository institutions bid every two weeks for a predetermined amount of funding that is repayable in 28 days.

On March 11, 2008, the Federal Reserve established a term auction funding facility, known as the **Term Securities Lending Facility** for primary dealers.[19] Five days later, the Federal Reserve created an overnight funding facility, known as the **Primary Dealer Credit Facility** for primary dealers.

Banks and primary dealers have readily used these new facilities as other sources of funding liquidity have become more costly and difficult to secure. This has greatly changed the composition of the assets on the Federal Reserve's balance sheet (see Table 3).

BEAR STEARNS

On Thursday March 13, 2008, Bear Stearns executives informed the Federal Reserve and the Securities and Exchange Commission that Bear Stearns' funding liquidity position had deteriorated during the week from $18 billion on Monday to $2 billion on Thursday. Unless alternative funding could be arranged, Bear Stearns would have to file for bankruptcy the next day. Lacking the financial intelligence about Bear Stearns that supervision would have provided, the Federal Reserve was blindsided by this declaration.

A bankruptcy court would have frozen all liabilities of Bear Stearns for months while the bankruptcy proceedings unfolded. With billions of dollars owed to banks and other financial institutions through repos and lines of credits, an extended freeze could have caused extreme credit losses in many other financial institutions, possibly leading to a global financial meltdown of catastrophic portions.

Although the FDIC can resolve a failing bank overnight to avoid the freeze problem inherent in bankruptcy, there is no quick resolution alternative to bankruptcy for highly leveraged non-depository financial institutions. This lacuna prompted the Federal Reserve to exercise its emergency lending power and arrange the involuntary acquisition of Bear Stearns by JPMorgan-Chase.

On Friday March 14, 2008, the Federal Reserve arranged a 28-day line of credit through JPMorganChase. Over the weekend, JPMorgan-Chase agreed to acquire Bear Stearns for $2 per share, a small fraction of what its shares were valued early in the week. The Federal Reserve agreed to take up to $30 billion of securities owned by Bear Stearns onto its books. To avoid shareholder litigation, JPMorgan-Chase subsequently increased its offer to $10 per share. JPMorgan-Chase also agreed to compensate the Federal Reserve for any losses on its portfolio of former Bear Stearns assets up to $1 billion dollars.

FISCAL RESPONSE

On February 13, 2008, President George W. Bush signed the *Recovery Rebates and Economic Stimulus for the American People Act of 2008*. The act:

- Provides a refundable 10 percent rebate on the first $6,000 of taxable income ($12,000 for couples) that is phased out at a 5 percent rate for incomes over $75,000 ($150,000 for couples) plus an additional $300 per qualifying child if eligible for a rebate;
- Allows 50 percent bonus depreciation for business purchases of qualifying equipment in 2008;
- Increases the amount of eligible investment (generally equipment) expensing from $128,000 to $250,000 and the phase-out threshold from $510,000 to $800,000 for 2008;

Table 3. Federal Reserve Bank Assets (in Millions)

	6-27-07	Percent	6-18-08	Percent
U.S. Treasuries	$790,497	87.6%	$478,734	51.0%
Repurchase Agreements	$20,000	2.2%	$133,500	14.2%
Term Auction Credit	$0	0.0%	$150,000	16.0%
Discounts to Deposito-ry Institutions	$187	0.0%	$13,744	1.5%
Discounts to Primary Dealers	$0	0.0%	$8,145	0.9%
Float	-$152	0.0%	-$1,781	-0.2%
Other Assets	$40,233	4.5%	$103,820	11.1%
Gold Stock	$11,041	1.2%	$11,041	1.2%
SDR	$2,200	0.2%	$2,200	0.2%
Treasury Currency	$38,526	4.3%	$38,833	4.1%
Off-Balance Sheet – Like Securities Lent to Primary Dealers				
Overnight Facility	*$0*	*0.0%*	*$4,361*	*0.5%*
Term Facility	*$0*	*0.0%*	*$114,457*	*12.2%*

- Increases the conforming mortgage loan limits for Fannie Mae and Freddie Mac up to $729,750 for loans originated between July 1, 2007 and December 31, 2008; and
- Allows the Federal Housing Administration (FHA) to insure mortgages in high-cost areas up to $729,750 through December 31, 2008.

REGULATORY RESPONSE

To date, the major thrust has been to assist delinquent subprime borrowers in refinancing their residential mortgage loans on more favorable terms and to provide more liquidity in the RMBS market through Fannie Mae and Freddie Mac.

On October 10, 2007, Secretary of the Treasury Henry Paulson announced the administration had brokered an alliance, known as HOPE Now, among mortgage bankers, RMBS issuers, servicers, counselors, and investors. This Alliance issued a statement that identifies subprime mortgagers that are in danger of defaulting and outlines refinancing, loan modifications, and loss mitigation steps consistent with the governing Pooling and Service Agreements for the RMBS or CMOs into which these mortgages have been placed. Through April 2008, 1.56 million home owners have arranged work-out plans through the HOPE Now program.[20]

The Bush administration created the FHA Secure program to help households refinance their adjustable-rate subprime mortgage loans if the borrowers fell behind in payments after a rate adjustment. Subprime borrowers that qualify can refinance through a fixed-rate FHA-insured residential mortgage loan up to 97.5 percent of the current market value of their residence. Over 100,000 home owners have benefited from the FHA Secure program.[21]

On March 19, 2008, the Office of Housing Finance Enterprise Oversight announced that it lowered the capital surplus requirements for Fannie Mae and Freddie Mac from 30 percent to 20 percent. This change allows Fannie Mae and Freddie Mac to purchase up to $200 billion of RMBS and tranches of CMOs.

Global Credit Losses and Likely Effects on U.S. Economy

The U.S. housing bubble and resulting global financial crisis have harmed the American economy. In April 2008, the IMF forecast that the global credit losses from the financial crisis will be $945 billion (which is equivalent to 6.83 percent of U.S. GDP in 2007).[22] These massive credit losses have triggered a severe credit crunch as banks rehabilitate their balance sheets. Despite the extraordinary measures taken by the Federal Reserve, the IMF estimates that this credit crunch will reduce U.S. real GDP by 1.4 percentage points below what it would have otherwise been for up to three quarters.[23]

The Federal Reserve reported that declining U.S. housing prices reduced owners' equity in residential real estate in the household and nonprofit sector by 8.8 percent from its peak of $9.997 trillion on March 31, 2007 to $9.1 17 trillion on March 31, 2008. This loss contributed to a 3.8 percent reduction in the net worth of the household and non-profit sector from its peak of $58.2 trillion on September 30, 2007 to $56.0 trillion on March 31, 2008.[24] The negative wealth effect on consumption expenditures by households due to declining net worth is likely to remain a drag on economic growth so long as housing prices continue to decline.

Conclusion

This chapter investigates the development of an alternative financial system to the traditional bank-centric system during the last three decades. This alternative financial system, which is based upon securitization and highly leveraged non-depository financial institutions, performs the same economically vital, but inherently risky functions of intermediation and liquidity and maturity transformation that the traditional bank-centric system does without the same safeguards. The vulnerabilities of this alternative financial system to a modern version of bank runs and financial contagion became apparent during the global financial crisis that began on August 9, 2007.

The report also examines the global financial crisis and the response from federal policymakers. The opacity inherent in structured credit products and the lack of supervision of HLNDFIs slowed the recognition of the gravity of the global financial crisis. However, federal policymakers have generally responded appropriately once its severity became apparent.

Since the Fed-assisted acquisition of Bear Stearns by JPMorgan-Chase in March 2008, funding liquidity for most banks, other depository institutions, and HLNDFIs has improved, and the elevated spreads in credit markets have eased somewhat.

End Notes

[1] Robert P. O'Quinn, *The U.S. Housing Bubble and the Global Financial Crisis: Housing and Housing-Related Finance* (Prepared for the Joint Economic Committee, 110 Cong., 2nd sess., May 2008). Found at: http://www.house.gov/jec/news/Housing%20Bubble%20study.pdf.

[2] Charles P. Kindleberger devised a seven-stage framework of assets bubbles. See generally, Charles P. Kindleberger, *Manias, Panics, and Crashes: A History of Financial Crises* (1978; 4th ed., New York: John Wiley & Sons, 2000).

[3] Structured finance refers to the pooling of credit risk from multiple borrowers into a different credit product.

[4] Finance companies are non-depository financial firms that lend to consumers and non-financial firms.

[5] Financial government-sponsored enterprises (GSEs) are financial institutions that provide credit to specific groups or economic sectors. Financial GSEs include the Federal Home Loan Banks, Fannie Mae, Freddie Mac, Sallie Mae (Student Loan Marketing Association, since 1997 a subsidiary of SLM Holding Corporation, a private company), the Farm Credit System, Financing Corporation (FICO), and Resolution Funding Corporation (REFCORP).

[6] Hedge funds are private investment companies that are open only to qualified investors to avoid regulation under the *Investment Company Act of 1940*.

[7] Investment banks are security/broker dealers.

[8] Off-balance sheet entities (OBSEs) are asset-backed commercial paper (ABCP) conduits and special investment vehicles (SIVs) sponsored by banks. See *World Economic and Financial Surveys, Global Financial Stability Report: Containing Systemic Risk and Restoring Financial Soundness* (Washington, D.C.: International Monetary Fund, April 2008), 70-72.

[9] A "repo" is a repurchase agreement in which one party sells securities to a second party with an agreement to repurchase these securities at a fixed higher price on a specified future date (usually overnight). This is essentially a loan with the interest rate implied by the difference between the sale price and the higher repurchase price. A "reserve repo" is a reserve repurchase agreement in which one party purchases specific securities from a second party with an agreement to resell these securities at a fixed higher price at a specific future date (usually overnight). This is essentially a security loan with the interest rate implied by the difference between the purchase price and the higher sale price.

[10] Federal Reserve Flow of Funds statistics for September 30, 2007, and IMF estimates for hedge funds and OBSEs.

[11] Leverage ratios in hedge funds vary tremendously from as little as 2.0:1 to as much as 30.0:1.

[12] Under the Basel II capital standards, the regulatory capital ratio for banks refers to the ratio of either Tier I or Tier II capital to risk-weighted assets. Tier I capital includes common stock, perpetual, non-cumulative preferred stock, and retained earnings. Tier II capital includes all items in Tier I capital plus undisclosed reserves, revaluation reserves, general and specific credit loss reserves, hybrid debt-capital instruments and subordinated term debt with a term

of five years or more. Under Basel II, risk- weighted assets may be calculated through a standard formula (for small banks) or through an internal rating approach (for large banks).

[13] The eight federal agencies are (1) Board of Governors of the Federal Reserve System (Federal Reserve), (2) Commodity Futures Trading Commission (CFTC), (3) Federal Deposit Insurance Corporation (FDIC), (4) National Credit Union Administration (NCUA), (5) Office of Federal Housing Enterprise Oversight (OFHEO), (6) Office of the Comptroller of the Currency (OCC), (7) Office of Thrift Supervision (OTC), and (8) Securities and Exchange Commission (SEC).

[14] Insurance is regulated by insurance commissioners in each state instead of the federal government.

[15] *Global Financial Stability Report* (April 2008), 59-64.

[16] Federal Deposit Insurance Corporation, *Quarterly Banking Profile* (First Quarter 2008).

[17] The average risk-weighted Tier I capital ratio for all U.S. banks and savings institutions fell from 10.4 percent on June 30, 2007 to 10.1 percent on March 31, 2008. FDIC.

[18] Board of Governors of the Federal Reserve System, *Senior Loan Officer Survey on Bank Lending Practices* (January 2008). Found at: http://www.federalreserve.gov/boarddocs/SnLoanSurvey/200801/table1.htm.

[19] A primary dealer is a bank or securities broker-dealer that may trade directly with the Federal Reserve.

[20] HOPE Now website.

[21] Department of Housing and Urban Development. Found at: http://www.hud.gov/news/release.cfm?content=pr08-024.cfm.

[22] *Global Financial Stability Report* (2008), 10.

[23] Ibid., 35.

[24] Federal Reserve/Haver. Percent calculation by author.

In: Economic Crises as a Result of Distrust
Editors: Emilio Gullini
ISBN: 978-1-60741-355-4

Chapter 10

How the Credit Crisis Affects You

Charles E. Schumer and Carolyn B. Maloney

Overview

We are all familiar with the numerous ways in which we use credit. Credit finances the smaller purchases we make when we use our credit cards, and the larger purchases that are fundamental to our lives – the cars we drive, the homes we live in, the colleges where we send our children. Credit is also crucial for the needs of businesses, and for state and local governments.

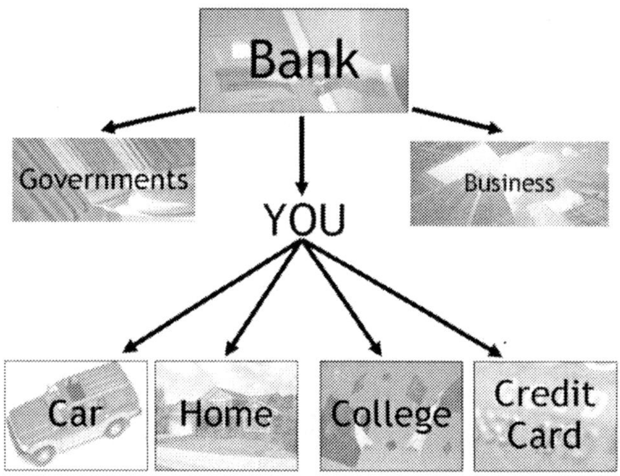

At its most basic level, credit is what allows us to make purchases today based on the money we are going to earn in the future. When we purchase a car or a house, few of us have the full cash amount available, so we borrow money from a lender who has confidence in our ability to repay the loan (plus interest) over time. This enables us to turn our future earnings into current spending, and in turn, furthers economic growth by increasing demand for the goods we are purchasing. If people could only buy cars when they had saved up the full purchase price, there would be many fewer cars sold, and many fewer people employed in every facet of the auto industry.

In the same way, institutional actors also depend on credit. Businesses rely on credit to get off the ground (leasing space, buying start up equipment), to keep their operations running (stocking their shelves, buying new equipment, making payroll and paying the electric bill) and they use credit to expand (opening new stores and factories, and hiring new employees).Government also relies on credit to pay for many of their longer term projects—school improvements, highway repairs, new streetlights—which they finance by issuing bonds against future tax revenues.

In today's economy, all of these forms of credit are part of a much larger global financial web, in which financial institutions around the world are constantly borrowing and lending to one another, to manufacturers and retailers, and, ultimately, to consumers. In short, while we may not always see it, credit is the lifeblood of the economy.

How the Credit Crisis Fuels Economic Slowdown

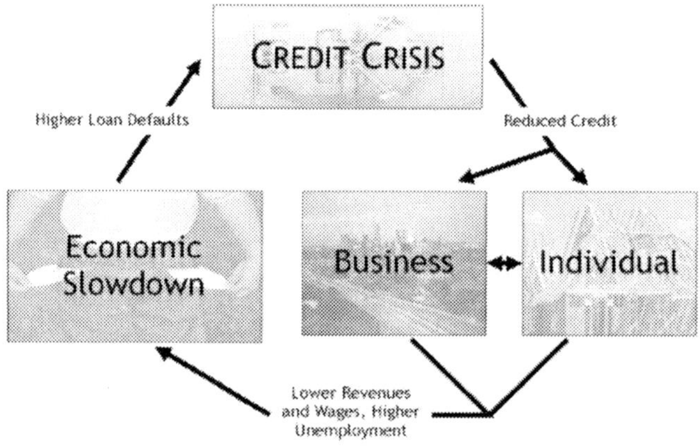

At its most extreme, the availability of credit can dry up, and a credit crisis, such as we are now experiencing, can occur. When a credit crisis does occur, the consequences for the economy can be devastating. The lack of available credit forces individuals and businesses alike to cut back on spending, reducing business revenues, which then causes wages to drop and unemployment to rise. The resulting economic slowdown causes more individuals and businesses to default on their loans, worsening the credit crisis. In short, this is a vicious circle, in which a credit freeze and economic contraction feed into each other.

THE ONSET OF THE CREDIT CRISIS

The Securitization of Loans

Over the past decade, credit was increasingly "securitized". Banks would pool together many different loans, and then sell securities, based on the rights to the payments from the loans in the pool, to outside investors. The sales of these securities provided banks with immediate cash, which they could then use to make more mortgages. And investors liked these securities, because they were considered safe investments (frequently, nearly as safe as U.S. Treasury bills, and they typically paid a higher return than equivalent investments).

From Your House to Wall Street

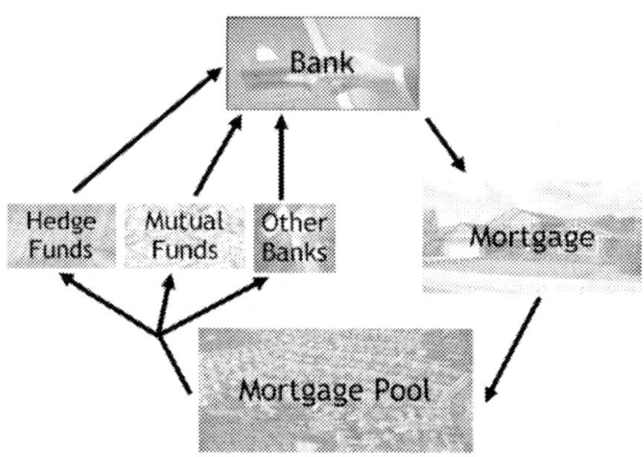

The most common and well-known of these securitized loans is the "mortgage-backed security" (MBS), based on pools of residential mortgages. But many other types of loans have also increasingly become securitized over the past decade—car loans, student loans, even credit card debt. Over the past decade, this type of securitized credit saw explosive growth, because of the superior returns and perception of safety. By the first quarter of 2006, the total value of all outstanding U.S. MBS totaled approximately $6.1 trillion.

The Deflation of the Housing Bubble

As is now obvious, the U.S. experienced an unprecedented housing bubble in the earlier part of this decade. The availability of easy, cheap credit with low underwriting standards inflated the demand for housing, which led to increased housing prices. The growing housing market made mortgage-backed securities increasingly attractive, creating more demand among investors for MBS, which then provided even more credit for US homebuyers. This housing bubble has now officially popped. But the repercussions for the US economy have not yet been fully felt.

The deflation of the housing bubble has brought increased mortgage defaults which, coupled with concerns about poor mortgage underwriting standards, and the widespread belief that U.S. housing prices are still overvalued, have led to tremendous declines in the values of MBS. And because MBS—and other forms of securitized debt—were so widely held, some major financial institutions have been forced to take huge writedowns in recent months.

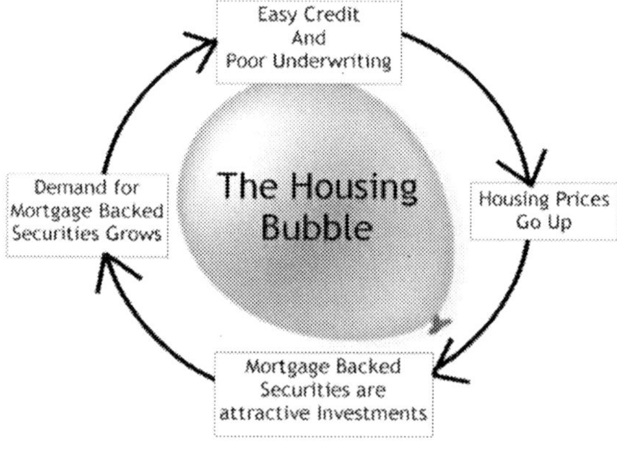

As these writedowns have become recognized, these financial institutions have been forced to raise capital to cover the losses incurred. Those which have been able to raise sufficient capital have so far been able to survive, while those which have been unable to raise sufficient capital have failed, sometimes suddenly and unexpectedly.

Large Financial Institutions Fail Overnight

Bear Stearns was one of the first major examples of a big failure of a financial firm, due to its inability to find sufficient capital to cover its mortgage related losses. In March 2008, the Federal Reserve negotiated a deal in which JP Morgan Chase acquired Bear Stearns at an extremely low price ($10/share), which only happened because of the inclusion of federal guarantees on some $30 billion in risky Bear Stearns assets. The collapse of Bear Stearns began a steady deterioration in credit conditions, during which time a number of banks failed, which came to a head in September.

The weekend of September 13-14, the eminent Wall Street firm Merrill Lynch, concerned about its ability to survive future MBS losses, agreed to sell itself to Bank of America for considerably less than where its stock price had stood a few months earlier. That same weekend, Lehman Brothers, another iconic Wall Street firm, was unable to obtain any relief, and so was forced to file for bankruptcy on September 15.

Both Merrill and Lehman came under heavy pressure because they possessed insufficient capital. As mortgage-related losses mounted, customers began pulling out of brokerage accounts with Merrill and Lehman, concerned about the safety of their assets. Merrill and Lehman thus came under increasing pressure to raise more capital to cover these losses and the outflows of brokerage deposits. When it became apparent that the capital available was insufficient to cover their expected losses, Merrill sold itself to Bank of America, and Lehman entered into bankruptcy.

Around this same time, AIG, the world's largest insurance company, also came under heavy pressure to raise capital. AIG's financial arm, AIG Financial Products, had accrued an enormous amount of exposure to mortgage - related assets, and as a result, it was carrying enormous unrecognized losses on its books. On September 15, the day Lehman announced bankruptcy, AIG's auditors forced AIG to recognize some of these losses. As a result, the next day, September 16, AIG was forced to effectively sell 80% of its equity to the Federal Reserve in exchange for an $85 billion line of credit.

These events were widely considered shocking. Many observers felt that Lehman could survive, and its inability to find any capital to save itself was an eye-opening event. The demises of Merrill and AIG were even more sobering, because they were widely considered to be in sterling shape up until a few days before their dispositions.

Confidence in the Health of Financial Institutions Drops, Causing Credit Freeze Among Banks

Finding credit was already difficult in this environment, but the sudden and unexpected failures of Lehman Brothers and AIG caused lending to freeze up even more. Lehman in particular caused problems, because many investors which had uninsured accounts with, or other exposure to, Lehman, suddenly lost the ability to access their cash, with no idea of how much, if anything, they would be able to eventually recover.

Confidence in the solvency of financial institutions has plummeted and as a result, banks virtually ceased lending to one another. The most widely-used measure of lending between banks (the London interbank overnight rate or "LIBOR"), reached an all-time high of 6.88% this past Tuesday (September 30), an indication that banks are extremely reluctant to lend to each other at any interest rate. This is an indication of the extreme lack of confidence banks have in the financial system right now.

Other Sources of Credit Also Freezing Up

In addition to bank lending, other sources of credit have also dried up. Money market mutual funds, which are considered safe alternatives to depository accounts, have also come under serious pressure in recent weeks. Money market funds have historically been an important source of credit for businesses, as they are a major purchaser of short-term corporate debt (also called "commercial paper").

Following the failure of Lehman, two money market funds failed due to their exposure to Lehman debt. This is unprecedented. Money market funds, which are not federally insured, have historically been extremely safe and conservative, with their sole goal being to break even. From 1971 up to

September 2008, there was only one money market fund which failed. These failures led to a run on money market funds, which has continued to this time, as investors have withdrawn their money. On Monday (September 29), money market funds saw a $10 billion outflow of funds.

The decline in money market funds has already caused corporate borrowing costs to skyrocket. Short-term corporate debt rates jumped from 2% on Monday to a range between 5.75% and 7.75% on Tuesday.

The problems in money market funds signal larger problems in the debt markets. Corporate and municipal bond issues are becoming costlier and harder to fulfill. Even such long-time institutions as GE, AT&T, and the State of Massachusetts are finding it difficult to find enough buyers of their bond issues.

HOW WILL THE CREDIT CRUNCH IMPACT ME?

So how will the credit crisis affect ordinary Americans, living outside the confines of Wall Street? It all goes back to the idea of the "vicious circle". As credit tightens up, Main Street businesses and consumers are forced to reduce spending. This in turn reduces the revenues of businesses, forcing them to cut costs, including lowering wages and cutting staff. As a result, businesses and individuals alike have more trouble paying their bills and are more likely to miss payments on their loans (like mortgages and corporate debt).

As these missed payments turn into loan defaults, the value of mortgage-backed securities and corporate debt is further reduced, which then forces Wall Street firms to cut back even further on their lending activities, causing a further tightening of credit.

In short, what we are seeing now, if uninterrupted is a feedback loop, where tighter credit leads to less economic activity, which leads to a decline in the value of financial assets, which then creates even tighter credit conditions. In an environment like the current one, only those borrowers with the safest credit ratings can find credit, and even this is costly. And without credit, businesses large and small wither and die. Whether it's the small business owner who cannot expand or the large conglomerate that cannot make payroll, the impact is the same – the economy shrinks and the pie gets smaller.

We are already seeing evidence that the vicious circle is well underway. Unemployment numbers are up again, with 159,000 newly unemployed workers in September. Auto sales have declined for 11 straight months, due to more restrictive credit and decreased consumer confidence, and as a result,

18% of US car dealerships may close in 2009. Private student lending has become severely restricted, as banks are increasingly unwilling to commit cash to long-term loans. And some colleges have already lost access to funds parked with failed institutions such as Wachovia and Lehman, which may ultimately raise the cost of tuition.

The impacts of the credit crisis are not limited to the private sector, either. Cities and states have become increasingly reliant on the issuance of bonds to finance various projects. Like other credit markets, the markets for "muni bonds" (which have historically been much safer than private bonds and offer significant tax benefits) have also frozen up. In recent weeks, a high number of municipalities, including Massachusetts, have been forced to back out of the muni bond market due to insufficient investor interest or overly high costs. One expert recently predicted that muni bond issuances would drop by 25-30% in 2009. Even those that are issued will almost certainly be at much higher cost, limiting the amount of new road construction, school maintenance, and other municipal and state projects that can be paid for.

The Vicious Cycle

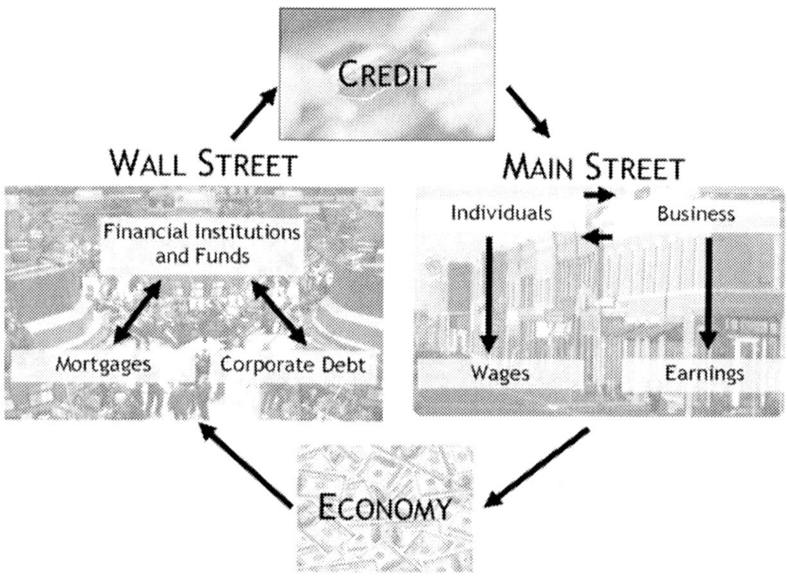

Non-profit institutions have in recent years also made extensive use of short-term borrowing, and like their for-profit analogues, they are already experiencing problems because of the credit freeze. Blood banks, hospitals, homeless shelters are among the many types of non-profit institutions that rely on the credit markets to meet their short funding needs. If the availability of credit continues to deteriorate, many of these non-profit entities will have to cut back, or even shut down.

How Will the Emergency Economic Stabilization Act Help the Credit Crisis?

The newly enacted Emergency Economic Stabilization Act (EESA) will help to alleviate the credit crisis by paying a fair price for the MBS that financial firms are currently holding. By adding a massive new buyer to the equation, EESA is expected to improve the market for MBS. Struggling financial firms can then sell some of their troubled assets, thus improving the condition of their balance sheets, and making it easier for them to attract new capital. More capital and less troubled assets will hopefully stimulate new lending.

However, the effects of EESA will not be known until the Treasury plan has been put into operation. While EESA may help to stabilize the credit markets, banks and other financial institutions may still require significant capital. Moreover, recent signs indicate that the real economy is beginning to slow significantly. Additional policy steps, including more stimulus, may be required in the near future.

In: Economic Crises as a Result of Distrust
Editors: Emilio Gullini
ISBN: 978-1-60741-355-4

Chapter 11

POLICY LESSON'S FROM JAPAN'S LOST DECADE

Jim Saxton

Japan experienced large asset price bubbles in its stock and commercial real estate markets during the second half of the 1980s. These bubbles peaked in 1989 and 1990, respectively. Subsequently, both Japanese share prices and land values fell, surrendering all of their gains during the bubble years by 1993 and 2000, respectively.

After these bubbles popped, real GDP growth slowed abruptly. However, a series of fiscal and monetary blunders by the Japanese government transformed the inevitable post-bubble recession into a "lost decade" of deflation and stagnation. U.S. policymakers can learn valuable lessons of what to do and not to do by studying these blunders.

SOWING SEEDS

During the second half of the 1980s, Japan enjoyed both rapid economic growth and low inflation (as recorded in price indices for goods and services). The Japanese yen appreciated from ¥260/US$ in February 1985 to a then all-time high of ¥150/US$ during the summer of 1986. Fearing a loss of price competitiveness for Japanese manufactured exports in the United States, the Japanese government changed the thrust of its economic policy from non-inflationary real GDP growth in Japan to containing the appreciation of the yen relative to the U.S. dollar.

Despite a booming economy, the Bank of Japan loosened its monetary policy to stem the appreciation of the yen by reducing its policy interest rate in steps from 5.0 percent in January 1986, to 2.5 percent in February 1987. This overly accommodative monetary policy fueled unsustainable price bubbles in the Japanese stock and commercial real estate markets.

To prick these bubbles, the Bank of Japan began to tighten its monetary policy, raising its policy interest rate from 2.5 percent in May 1989 in steps to a peak of 6.0 percent in August 1990. This tightening caused these bubbles to pop:

- The Nikkei 225 index, which was 13,000 at the end of 1985, peaked at 38,916 on the last trading day of 1989 and then fell by one-half in 1990. By 1993, all of the gains in share prices since 1985 had been eliminated. The Nikkei 225 index declined to a post-bubble low of 11,820 on March 13, 2001.
- The urban land price index rose by 199 percent from 35.1 in September 1985 to a peak of 105.1 in September 1990. The index then gradually declined over the next ten years to 34.6 percent in September 2000, eliminating all of the gains in real estate prices since 1985.

The collapse of these bubbles wrecked Japanese banks and other depository institutions:

- Japanese banks and other depository institutions were allowed to invest directly in stocks. The unrealized capital gains on these shares fell from ¥49.1 trillion ($355 billion) in 1989 to ¥5 trillion ($42 billion) in 2001, reducing bank capital.
- Japanese banks and other depository institutions secured almost all of their commercial and industrial loans through commercial real estate mortgages. As commercial real estate values escalated, credit standards deteriorated. Instead of examining whether non-financial firms could service their loans out of their cash flow from operations, Japanese banks and other depository institutions increasingly relied on rapidly escalating collateral values for repayment. Weak credit standards during the bubble years boosted problem loans and credit losses in Japanese banks and other depository institutions during the lost decade.

This weakness in Japanese banks and other depository institutions had especially devastating effects on the non-financial business sector in Japan because Japanese non-financial firms were more dependent on bank loans than their counterparts in the United States and other developed countries during the 1980s:

- Japanese non-financial firms generally had higher debt-to-equity ratios than their U.S. or European counterparts.
- The Japanese corporate debt market was relatively shallow. With less ability to issue commercial paper and corporate bonds, Japanese multinational firms (MNFs) relied more heavily on bank loans to finance investment than U.S. and European MNFs.
- Many Japanese non-financial firms, whose primary operations had nothing to do with real estate development, began speculating on commercial real estate as the bubble inflated. Widespread speculation devastated the balance sheets of these firms after the commercial real estate bubble popped.

BANKING CRISIS

Once these bubbles burst, Japanese banks and other depository institutions were saddled with mountains of non-performing loans. At first, the Japanese government played for time through a policy of forbearance. Japanese banks and other depository institutions delayed recognizing their losses on non-performing loans to insolvent non-financial firms. Instead, Japanese banks and other depository institutions continued lending to insolvent non-financial firms to keep them from filing for bankruptcy. This lending expanded the size of the non-performing loan problems at Japanese banks and other depository institutions during the first half of the 1990s.

By the middle 1990s, unrealized stock losses, loan charge-offs, and write-downs depleted the capital of many Japanese banks and other depository institutions. The failure of several *jusen* (specialized housing lenders) in 1995 forced the Japanese government to abandon its policy of forbearance.

Instead of forbearance, the Japanese government encouraged Japanese banks and other depository institutions to (1) "stop throwing good money after bad" and (2) charge-off non-performing loans to insolvent non-financial firms. Cumulative loan charge-offs from 1995 to 2003 were ¥37.2 trillion ($318 billion). Despite these loan charge-offs, non-performing loans did not peak until 2002 when they reached ¥43.2 trillion ($330 billion), or 8.4 percent of total loans.

The Japanese government also decided to (1) provide taxpayer funds to aid capital-impaired banks and other depository institutions, and (2) assist stronger banks to acquire failing banks and other depository institutions. Because of widespread public opposition, however, this policy of government assistance and consolidation proceeded in fits and starts. Over the next decade, the Japanese government provided total assistance of ¥46.8 trillion ($399 billion) to Japanese banks and other depository institutions through grants, asset purchases, equity injections, and other means. As of March 31, 2007, ¥22.8 trillion ($195 billion) of this assistance has been recovered.

Although this policy of government assistance and consolidation cost Japanese taxpayers ¥24.0 trillion ($204 billion), it worked. Japan now has a handful of well capitalized banks and other depository that are capable of providing the credit to Japanese households and firms necessary for sustained economic growth.

Lost Decade

As the financial condition of Japanese banks and other financial institutions deteriorated, credit for both entrepreneurs and new ventures of existing non-financial firms became scarce. Japanese non-financial firms slashed their research and development expenditures, retarding the diffusion of new technologies. These factors slowed productivity gains and stymied real GDP growth.

In July 1991, the Bank of Japan began to loosen its monetary policy. The Bank of Japan reduced its policy interest rate in steps to 0.5 percent by year-end 1995. As its policy interest rate approached zero, the Bank of Japan engaged in quantitative easing. Nevertheless, the real GDP growth rate stalled, averaging only 0.7 percent from 1992 to 1994, and disinflation morphed into deflation. This accommodative monetary policy failed to spark real GDP growth because:

- Weighed down with non-performing loans, Japanese banks and other depository institutions were unwilling to extend new loans to non-financial firms despite very low funding costs; and
- Japanese non-financial firms wanted to reduce their leverage and repair their balance sheets before borrowing additional funds to expand their operations.

As for fiscal policy, the Japanese government tried to stimulate real GDP growth by increasing infrastructure spending from 6.5 percent of GDP in 1990 to 8.3 percent of GDP in 1996. Instead of boosting real GDP growth, additional infrastructure spending actually hurt the Japanese economy:

- Since the Japanese government had spent far more on infrastructure as a percent of GDP than the United States or other developed countries, Japan had very few unfunded infrastructure projects that would increase productivity.
- In Japan, the choice of infrastructure projects is highly politicized and prior to 2002 was made without any cost-benefit analysis. Japanese politicians have traditionally competed for Diet seats based on their ability to "bring home the bacon" especially to rural constituencies. As a result, Japanese infrastructure projects are notoriously wasteful (e.g., rural roads with little traffic, bridges to islands with few residents, and expensive seldom-used harbor facilities for small fishing villages).
- Japanese construction firms are very inefficient compared with their counterparts in the United States and other developed countries. Infrastructure spending channeled taxpayer funds to one of Japan's least efficient sectors.
- Japanese politicians and political parties are heavily dependent on contributions from Japanese construction firms, while Japanese construction firms are heavily dependent on public infrastructure projects. This co-dependency has caused numerous "pay to play" scandals involving large illegal campaign contributions and payoffs from construction firms to policymakers.

The exposure of these scandals and widespread waste in infrastructure spending by the Japanese media forced the government to reverse its policy in 1997. By 2004, infrastructure spending fell to 4.8 percent of GDP.

When infrastructure spending did not spark a recovery, the Japanese government implemented temporary income tax reductions in 1994. These reductions boosted real GDP growth to 2.8 percent in 1996. However, concerns about Japanese government budget deficits caused the government to couple these temporary income tax reductions with a permanent increase in the consumption tax from 3 percent to 5 percent, effective April 1, 1997. After this permanent tax increase was implemented, real GDP contracted at an annualized rate of 3.3 percent in the second quarter of 1997, and real GDP continued to shrink in both 1998 and 1999.

Moreover, this tax increase did not reduce the Japanese government budget deficit. Instead, it rose from 3.8 percent of GDP in Japanese fiscal year 1997 to 7.2 percent of GDP in Japanese fiscal year 1999.

DIFFERENCES

Before discussing lessons learned, it is important to observe several important differences between the Japanese experience and the current situation confronting U.S. policymakers:

1. The asset price bubbles in the Japanese stock and commercial real estate markets were country-specific. The residential real estate bubble was global, occurring simultaneously in the United States and many other developed countries with floating exchange rates, including Australia, Ireland, Spain, and the United Kingdom.
2. The Japanese policy to pursue an overly accommodative domestic monetary policy to contain the appreciation of the foreign exchange value of the yen caused the stock and commercial real estate price bubbles in Japan during the second half of the 1990s. The causes of the residential real estate bubbles in the United States and other developed countries with floating exchange rates are complex and involve many macroeconomic and microeconomic policy errors by both the U.S. government and foreign governments.[1]
3. In Japan, non-financial firms were overleveraged and had weak balance sheets, while the household sector was in better shape when the stock and commercial real estate bubbles popped. In the United States, households were overleveraged and had weak balance sheets, while the non-financial business sector was in better shape when the residential real estate bubble popped.
4. Japan maintained significant current account surpluses during the bubble years and the lost decade. The United States has run significant current account deficits.

LESSONS FOR U.S. POLICYMAKERS

The bursting of the stock and commercial real estate price bubble in Japan and the subsequent lost decade offers many lessons for U.S. policymakers during the current global financial crisis and recession:

1. A recession inevitably follows the popping of a large asset price bubble. However, policy decisions made during the recession will affect both (1) its severity, and (2) the trajectory of the economy following the recession.
2. The banking system must become financially healthy before a sustained expansion can occur. U.S. banks and other financial institutions recognized their losses more rapidly than Japanese banks and other financial institutions. Moreover, the U.S. government injected taxpayer funds into U.S. banks and other financial institutions during this financial crisis far more quickly than did the Japanese government during the lost decade.
3. The balance sheet of the economic sector (business or household) that suffered the most damage from the collapse of a large asset price bubble must be repaired before a sustained expansion can occur. In Japan, non-financial firms had to reduce investment and use their profits to reduce their debt and rebuilt their balance sheets during Japan's lost decade before sustained growth resumed. Now, financially stressed U.S. households must reduce consumption and increase their saving rate to reduce their debt and rebuild their balance sheets. Thus, any portion of federal income tax reductions or rebates that households save should not be regarded as a failed stimulus. Normal economic growth cannot resume until this structural adjustment in the U.S. household sector is complete. "Saved" federal tax relief may speed this necessary adjustment.
4. Unlike Japan, international imbalances were a major macroeconomic cause of the residential real estate price bubble in the United States and many other developed countries with floating exchange rates. The correction of these imbalances may require difficult international negotiations to limit the ability of national governments to manipulate exchange rates.
5. While temporary income tax reductions helped Japanese economy in 1995 and 1996, the simultaneously enacted permanent increase in the consumption tax to reduce the Japanese government budget deficit in 1997 extinguished the benefits of these temporary reductions, sending the Japanese economy back into a recession. The automatic termination of

the federal income tax reductions enacted in 2001 and 2003 on December 31, 2010, may diminish the stimulus from any temporary federal tax reductions or rebates during 2009 and 2010 and may further weaken the U.S. economy in 2011.

6. Additional infrastructure spending may not bolster either short-term or long-term economic growth. First, there are lengthy delays between when infrastructure projects are authorized and when actual construction starts. Because of such delays, the desired boost in employment may occur months after a recession is over. Second, the ability of infrastructure projects to increase productivity and real GDP growth are unequal. To boost productivity long-term growth, policymakers must carefully select which projects they fund to screen out "boondoggles." Such a thorough selection process and a rapid funding of infrastructure projects to create jobs during a recession are in conflict. A rush to approve a large number of infrastructure projects may lead to wasteful expenditures that do not increase productivity and boost real GDP growth over time.

End Notes

[1] Macroeconomic causes include the interaction between (1) the exchange rate policy of the People's Republic of China (PRC) and the shadow exchange rate policies of other Asian countries to keep the foreign exchange values of their currencies below market-clearing levels after the Asian Financial Crisis of 1997-1998, and (2) implementation by either practice or rule of inflation-targeting by the Federal Reserve and central banks in other developed countries with floating exchange rates. This interaction distorted price signals globally. Over time, these price distortions produced (1) overinvestment and malinvestment in finance and housing sectors in the United States and many other developed countries with floating exchange rates, and (2) overinvestment and malinvestment in the manufacturing sector in the PRC and many other Asian countries. Microeconomic causes include (1) lacunas in the Basel capital standards, (2) a fundamental conflict in the business model of credit rating agencies, (3) fundamental flaws in the "originate to securitize" model of residential mortgage finance, (4) the inherent mission conflict in Fannie Mae and Freddie Mac, and (5) various policies that promoted home ownership among low- to moderate-income households that were not able to shoulder these responsibilities.

In: Economic Crises as a Result of Distrust
Editors: Emilio Gullini
ISBN: 978-1-60741-355-4

Chapter 12

CREDIT DEFAULT SWAPS: FREQUENTLY ASKED QUESTIONS

Edward Vincent Murphy

SUMMARY

Credit default swaps are contracts that provide protection against default by third parties, similar to insurance. These financial derivatives are used by banks and other financial institutions to manage risk. The rapid growth of the derivatives market, the potential for widespread credit defaults (such as defaults for subprime mortgages), and operational problems in the over-the-counter (OTC) market where credit default swaps are traded, have led some policymakers to inquire if credit default swaps are a danger to the financial system and the economy. For example, the establishment of a conservatorship for the government sponsored enterprises (GSEs), Fannie Mae and Freddie Mac, in September 2008 potentially triggered credit default swap contracts with notional value exceeding $1.2 trillion. Processing and covering these commitments may be difficult. This chapter defines credit default swaps, explains their use by banks for risk management, and discusses the potential for systemic risk.

What is a Credit Default Swap?

Basically, in a credit default swap contract, one party promises to pay another party if a third party defaults. The more technical definition of a credit default swap is a bilateral derivative contract that transfers from one party to another the risk that a specified reference entity will experience a "credit event." (Credit events may include default, bankruptcy, restructuring, or credit rating downgrade).[1] Typically, the protection buyer pays a periodic fee to a protection seller in return for compensation if a reference entity experiences a credit event. The reference entity, such as a large firm that has issued a bond or a trust that has issued a mortgage-backed security (MB S), is not a party to the credit default swap contract. The original protection buyer does not need to have ever owned the reference debt being protected; therefore, it is not necessary for the protection buyer to realize an actual loss in order to be eligible for compensation if a credit event occurs. The maturity of the credit default swap does not have to match the maturity of the reference asset, that is, a 10-year bond may be protected by a credit default swap that provides protection for only one year.

How Are Credit Default Swaps Used?

Historically, credit derivatives were primarily used by banks to manage their credit exposure to large loan customers. Banks and other institutions transfer some or all of their credit risk to other parties through credit default contracts. Because the buyer is paying for protection against uncertain events, credit default swaps perform a similar economic function as insurance; however, there are differences. First, credit default swap contracts can be traded more easily than insurance policies. Second, the protection buyer need never have had any asset at risk in order to purchase the swap and does not have to experience an actual loss from the credit event in order to collect the payment. Because credit default swaps can be originated, bought, and sold by parties with no direct exposure to the reference asset, credit default swap markets are sometimes compared to gambling. However, a specialized lender that is "overexposed" in one economic sector may wish to participate in credit default swaps for bonds of firms in other economic sectors in order to manage risk; therefore, it can be difficult to distinguish "gambling" from diversification.

What Is an Example of a Credit Default Swap?

A financial institution buys a $1 million bond issued by a large manufacturing company. The financial institution wants to protect itself from the credit risk of the bond but wants to retain other features. The financial institution could pay a third party to protect the bond in case of a credit event, such as actual default, or merely a downgrade of the manufacturing company's bonds by a credit rating agency. For the sake of this example, assume the financial institution pays the protection seller $1,000 annually in return for a promise from the protection seller to pay the financial institution the cash value of the loss from the credit event (cash payout). The protection contract is a credit default swap and can be traded in derivatives markets.

In this scenario, trouble in the manufacturing industry causes a credit rating agency to lower the rating of the bonds after two years. As a result, the market value of the bonds falls by $12,000. In this case, the financial institution will have paid two $1,000 payments and had the value of its bond asset fall by $12,000. It would receive $12,000 from the protection seller. The net result for the financial institution is a loss of the value of the $2,000 in annual fees, rather than the $12,000 loss from the credit event. Note that the financial institution does not have to sell the bond at the new lower price and experience an actual loss in order to collect the credit default swap payment.

Although it is common practice to create a credit default swap that fully covers the loss due to the credit event, parties can contract for any payment they wish. In the example, the parties could have set the protection payment ahead of time, such as a $10,000 payment in case of the credit event, rather than the change in the value of the bond, $12,000. The parties may also contract for physical delivery of the reference asset (the bond) at a pre-specified price that has the same effect as protecting the protection buyer from loss in value.

What Is Notional Principal or Notional Amount?

In general, the notional principal, or notional amount, of a derivative contract is a hypothetical underlying quantity upon which interest rate or other payment obligations are computed. For a credit default swap, the notional principal is the reference amount set in the contract. Note that the notional amount is significantly different from the dollar value the credit default swap puts at risk. In the above example, the notional amount was $1 million but the promised payment amounted only to $12,000. The market value of a credit default swap is more closely linked to the relative values of the annual fee and the protection payment than to the notional amount. The aggregate notional amount of credit default swaps has grown significantly. According to the Bank of International Settlements (BIS), the total notional amount of credit default swaps was $57.9 trillion in December 2007. The gross market value of those swaps was $2.0 trillion, which was 3.5% of the notional amount.

What is a Reference Entity?

The reference entity in a credit default swap contract is the entity that is the subject of a credit event. In the above example, the reference entity is the manufacturing company because the trigger for the credit default swap is a change in the credit status of bonds it issued. Note that the manufacturing company is not a party to the credit default swap contract.

Who Participates in the Credit Default Swap Market?

Historically, banks have had the largest market share in credit default swaps, both as buyers of protection and as sellers of protection.[2] Other significant participants, both as buyers and sellers of protection, include securities firms, monoline insurance firms, and hedge funds. On a much smaller scale, pension funds, corporations, and mutual funds also participate.

What is the ISDA and What Does it Do?

The ISDA is the International Swaps and Derivatives Association. Created in 1985, ISDA is an industry organization that seeks to identify and reduce the sources of risk in the derivatives and risk management business. The organization provides information on best practices (such as standardized contract forms and documentation), industry surveys and statistics, amicus briefs in court cases, and similar information. The ISDA master agreement provides market participants one avenue to standardize contracts, agree on settlement procedures and terms, and limit the risk that counterparties will not be able to fulfill their obligations.

Do Credit Default Swaps Create Systemic Risk?

Although there is no single, agreed-upon definition of systemic risk, it generally refers to the risk that the financial system will multiply the problems of one institution to many other institutions, including those that are otherwise solvent and liquid. Systemic concerns of credit default swaps, like many financial derivatives, often refer to five attributes. First, derivatives could be used to increase the risk that banks and other financial intermediaries face, rather than transfer risk to parties in a better position to sustain risk. Second, the sellers of protection may not be adequately capitalized to honor their commitments if many defaults occur at the same time. Third, derivatives contracts are very complex and may be misused by inexperienced, though sophisticated, market participants. Fourth, the notional value of derivatives greatly exceeds bank capital, so a change in the value of credit default swaps could greatly weaken the capital of the banking system, triggering a significant contraction in lending for investment and consumer spending. Fifth, tracking counter party obligations in the market can create challenges for processing the trades and may overwhelm the system if defaults occur simultaneously on a wide scale.[3]

The five factors discussed above are not mutually exclusive. Leverage refers to the ratio of a firm's assets to its capital. Banking regulators impose regulatory and risk-based capital standards that limit leverage in the banking system. One use of a credit default swap is for banks, as protection buyers, to reduce the credit risk that they face. This could allow the banks to more easily meet their capital standards and increase their overall leverage. If protection sellers have not adequately prepared for losses, then a wave of credit events could overwhelm protection sellers, put in question their ability to honor their commitments, and lower the value of the credit default swaps held by the banks. Because the credit default swap market is so large relative to bank capital, the reduction in the value of the swaps could significantly damage the banking system. Similarly, if credit default swaps became difficult to trade, then their value according to mark-to-market accounting rules would have to be discounted, which could erode financial institution capital even if the institutions had no intention of selling them.

It may be the case that market participants and regulators have adequately prepared for the risks associated with credit default swaps. Those who take this position might argue that participants in the credit default swap market are overwhelmingly banks, hedge funds, and similar organizations that have access to highly sophisticated expertise. Similarly, these institutions are most aware of the potential risks in the credit default swap market. Others might respond that individual financial institutions might not have the incentive to fully prepare for the risks if they believe they will be aided in time of crisis.

How Have Credit Default Swaps Been Used in Securitization?

In securitization, debt instruments such as mortgages or auto loans are pooled into a trust and the resultant cash flow is sliced into tranches and sold to investors as securities. Credit default swaps have been used to (1) enhance the credit rating of individual tranches and (2) provide protection to originators who backstop the entire structure. In this case, backstop refers to originators who retain an equity position (first loss) in the structure, promise to repurchase or swap non-performing loans, or provide other credit enhancement for the securitization. In some cases, a first loss position might itself be securitized as a collateralized debt obligation (CDO) with its own set of tranches enhanced by credit default swaps. Problems in the housing markets have caused many credit events for mortgage-backed securities and providers of related credit default swaps, such as Ambac, have experienced some financial difficulties.[4]

Who Regulates Credit Default Swaps?

The over-the-counter market, where credit default swaps are traded, is not directly overseen by federal financial regulators. On the other hand, the use of credit default swaps by the institutions with the largest market share, banks, is regulated. More specifically, the risk management practices of banks are subject to direct supervision by the federal regulators who coordinate through the Federal Financial Institutions Examinations Council (FFIEC).[5] Use of credit default swaps and other complex derivatives is concentrated in the largest commercial banks, most of which are federally chartered institutions regulated by the Office of the Comptroller of the Currency (OCC), which is a member of FFIEC. Because the efficiency of the over-the-counter derivatives market affects the safety and soundness of federally chartered banks, the OCC "... spends a considerable amount of time and resources evaluating the risk control systems these banks use to manage risk in derivatives markets."[6]

The OCC is not the only institution with an interest in monitoring and proposing changes to credit default swaps and related markets. The Securities and

Exchange Commission (SEC), for example, has conducted notice and comment rulemaking for credit default swap options on the Chicago Board Options Exchange.[7] Also, the Federal Reserve Bank of New York has been working with the ISDA to facilitate the tracking of counterparty obligations.[8] In addition, private market participants have issued reports and made recommendations for the standardization and resolution of counterparty risk.[9]

How Did the Establishment of a Conservatorship for Fannie Mae and Freddie Mac Affect Credit Default Swaps?

The government-sponsored enterprises (GSEs), Fannie Mae and Freddie Mac, had combined debt exceeding $1.2 trillion when they were placed in a conservatorship by the Federal Housing Finance Agency. The ISDA has announced that it will publish a protocol to process credit default swaps that included a conservatorship for the GSEs as a triggering credit event.[10] The protocol will be open to members and non-members of ISDA. Credit default swaps related to the GSEs commonly included bankruptcy and restructuring (both of which could include conservatorship) as credit events, according to a working paper for the Office of Federal Housing Enterprise Oversight (now a part of the Federal Housing Finance Agency).[11]

End Notes

[1] Moorad Choudhry, "Credit Derivatives," *Handbook of Financial Instruments*, F. Fabozzi ed., (NJ: Wiley and Sons), 2002, pp. 790-797.

[2] "Credit Default Swaps - Into the Mainstream," *GE Asset Management*, spring 2005.

[3] For a discussion of operational issues in managing complex payment exchanges, see CRS Report RL33639, *Sources of Systemic Risk in Large Value Interbank Payment Systems*, by Edward Vincent Murphy.

[4] CRS Report RL34364, *Bond Insurers: Issues for the 110th Congress*, by Baird Webel and Darryl E. Getter.

[5] CRS Report RL33235, *Banking and Securities Regulation and Agency Enforcement Authorities*, by Mark Jickling, Gary Shorter, M. Maureen Murphy, and Michael V. Seitzinger.

[6] Testimony of Kathryn Dick, Deputy Comptroller for Credit and Market Risk, Before the Subcommittee on Securities, Insurance, and Market Risk of the Senate Committee on Banking, Housing, and Urban Affairs, July 9, 2008.

[7] Securities Exchange Act Release No. 34-55871 (June 6, 2007).

[8] "Statement Regarding June 9 Meeting on Over-the-Counter Derivatives," Press Release, Federal Reserve Bank of New York, June 9, 2008.

[9] One example is a study group formed by major investment banks and market makers, including Goldman Sachs & Co. and Citigroup, which issued *The Report of the Counterparty Risk Management Policy Group II*, July 27, 2005, available at [http://www.crmpolicygroup.org/].

[10] "ISDA to Publish Protocol for Fannie and Freddie," News Release, ISDA, September 8, 2008, available at [http://www.isda.org/].

[11] Robert Collender, "Enterprise Credit Default Swaps and Market Discipline: Preliminary Analysis," OFHEO Working Paper 08-2, July 2008, p. 3.

CHAPTER SOURCES

The following chapters have been previously published

Chapter 1 - This is an edited, reformatted and augmented version of remarks from Ranking Republican Member Jim Saxton before Joint Economic Committee United States Congress, Dated March 2008.

Chapter 2 - This is an edited, reformatted and augmented version of a Congressional Research Service publication, Report Order Code RS22961, Updated September 29, 2008.

Chapter 3 - This is an edited, reformatted and augmented version of a Congressional Research Service publication, CRS Report for Congress, The U.S. Financial Crisis: Lessons From Sweden.

Chapter 4 - This is an edited, reformatted and augmented version of a Congressional Research Service publication, Report Order Code R40007, Dated December 3, 2008.

Chapter 5 - This is an edited, reformatted and augmented version of remarks from Joint Economic Committee Research Report # 110-25, Dated September 2008.

Chapter 6 - This is an edited, reformatted and augmented version of remarks from Joint Economic Committee Research Report # 110-26, Dated October 2008.

Chapter 7 - This is an edited, reformatted and augmented version of remarks from Joint Economic Committee Research Report # 110-27, Dated October 2008.

Chapter 8 - This is an edited, reformatted and augmented version of remarks from Joint Economic Committee Research Report # 110-22, Dated May 22, 2008.

Chapter 9 - This is an edited, reformatted and augmented version of remarks from Joint Economic Committee Research Report # 110-23, Dated June 25, 2008.

Chapter 10 - This is an edited, reformatted and augmented version of remarks prepared by The Joint Economic Committee Majority Staff, Senator Charles E. Schumer, Chair, Rep. Carolyn B. Maloney, Vice Chair, Dated October 3, 2008.

Chapter 11 - This is an edited, reformatted and augmented version of remarks from Joint Economic Committee Research Report # 110-30, Dated December 2008.

Chapter 12 - This is an edited, reformatted and augmented version of a Congressional Research Service publication, Report Order Code RS22932, Updated September 9, 2008.

INDEX

A

B

C

D

E

F

G

N

O

P

Q

R

S

T

U

V

W

Y